A BETTER LIFE

How I Learned to Recover from Debilitating
Chronic Pain to Create a Life I Love

MONA MOSTOW

PART 1

LIFE INTERRUPTED

My Story

In the fall of 2011 I was living the life of a married, stay-at-home mom to my two children, Nathan, who was eleven at the time, and Olivia, who at two years younger than Nathan was nine. We were in the throes of baseball season, dance classes, middle school and elementary school. I had been a stay-at-home mom since the birth of my firstborn in March 2000. I *loved* being a stay-at-home mom. I couldn't imagine anyone else taking care of my son. My husband and I knew when we married and had kids that this was the plan from the start. It was a shared value. I liked my job well enough, but nothing was going to pull me away from my baby. When my daughter was born two and a half years later we became a happy little threesome while my husband was off at work. I filled their days to the max. We spent their younger years in weekly playgroups, playgrounds, the library, local recreation center classes, playdates, the pool and every local zoo and museum. We went home to nap and eat and spent the rest of our time out doing things. When they were old enough for school I spent most of my time overseeing activities. They had basketball, T-ball, soccer, dance classes, Little Gym and weekly playdates. If we were at home, I spent a *lot* of time reading to them. One of my favorite memories is sitting on the floor of their rooms and reading from an enormous pile of books while they sat on my lap. As the years went on my children became "specialists" in their desired activities. I believed they would "get behind" if they did not dedicate themselves completely to their activities. Encouraging our kids to start young and practice often seemed to be the road all of us moms were on—the majority anyway. I was what you would call a helicopter parent. I was obsessed with keeping my kids safe and doing the right thing. I was in a constant state of stress about their health, their progress at school and their placements in activities. Somewhere along the line this anxiety started showing itself in my life. I would have unexplained rashes, my heart rate would jump and stay up out of nowhere, especially when I'd lie down to sleep. Then that worry would turn into a full-blown panic attack. Why was I feeling this way?

Leading up to the fall of 2011 I got strep throat. I had had it before and knew the signs. At this time, my allergist was the doctor I was seeing most regularly for my asthma, so she did my test and treated me. The antibiotics she gave me were not working. The strep throat was almost gone, but not completely. My allergist sent me to an ear, nose and throat specialist (ENT) to talk about possibly removing my tonsils. When I met with this doctor she had a hard time believing I had strep because I looked fine and my tonsils looked fine. But the test was positive. I knew—I could feel it in my stomach. If you've ever had strep, you know you can feel it in your stomach and not in your throat at all. It shows up in different ways.

It had been weeks. So I got yet another antibiotic and the ENT scheduled surgery. By this time I was really worried. I felt like my throat was closing up every day, which then led me to be more anxious than ever.

An hour or two after I took the last antibiotic she gave me I started feeling itchy, and a few hours later my mouth felt itchy. I drove myself to the emergency room (ER) and was given a steroid to stop the allergic reaction. The ER doctor spoke to my ENT and they decided to give me Ciproflaxin.

Ciproflaxin is a black box medication that should be prescribed only in the most dire life-or-death situation. It also has horrific side effects including tendon pain, tendon ruptures, nerve pain and nerve damage, especially when taken with a steroid. Which is exactly what they sent me home with—a bottle of each. I really don't know if I was having a true allergic reaction. I was not processing anything well at that time. I could have been itchy from any number of things. And I'm not sure my mouth would have been itchy so much later in the day after taking it, or even itchy at all. But the combination of that and my throat feeling like it was closing was just too much for me to take. I panicked and drove myself to the ER.

That night I started to have a strange pain in my legs and of course I was wide awake with my heart pounding from the steroid. I got up in the morning feeling like I was hit by a bus, dizzy and my head swimming. I took another dose of each medication right before sending my kids off to school. Shortly after, I heard a loud buzzing in my head and a "pop" and next thing I knew I was on the floor. I had severe pain shooting through my legs and arms. I could hardly stand and was extremely dizzy. As soon as my kids got on the bus I called my mom hysterically crying. She was not yet retired and left work to find me on the floor of my living room. It was then I thought to look at the side effects of my medications. In the small print I read that Cipro can cause tendon and nerve damage, especially when taken with a steroid. I called my ENT immediately and explained to her what had happened. She told me to come in right away. My mom took me to her office, where all she really did was cancel my surgery. There was no follow-up on what had happened to me or on the instructions she gave the ER doctor that had put me in this condition. Both of them were negligent. I had years and years of anger toward them. But I never went after them legally because what was to come in the years ahead drained me of any energy to fight.

I was stunned this had happened. I kept waiting for the pain to go away. But it didn't. I needed to find someone else to help me, but I didn't even know where to start looking. I knew I needed some type of therapy and maybe a neurologist. In the meantime I went back to my allergist, who sent me down a road that left me confused and frustrated and honestly scared. I was so scared. Looking back now, it's obvious either she didn't know how to treat me (let's be real here—she was an allergist) or she was covering for the ENT she had sent me to. No doctor wants to put the blame on another doctor. However, some are honest and I found that to be true with the orthopedist I eventually found. More on that soon. The only good news out of this appointment was that my strep was gone. The Cipro certainly killed it along with my microbiome. But I wouldn't figure that out for a couple of years.

My allergist ordered a full blood panel to see if there was any other reason for the pain I was experiencing, and that's when the positive result came back for rheumatoid arthritis (RA). *Oh my, here we go.* And so began the divided lines between the doctors who thought my pain was from RA and those who believed it was a side effect of the drugs. I knew it was a side effect. But I also couldn't deny the blood test, so I agreed to see a rheumatologist. When I had a more specialized blood panel done at the rheumatologist's office, it showed I had markers for several autoimmune diseases, including Sjögren syndrome and lupus, in addition to the RA. So this meant more drugs. Another *steroid!* I went on Plaquenil, which is given to Sjögren patients. I was horrified to learn that drug can lead to blindness. I had to go to an ophthalmologist and have my vision thoroughly tested on a regular basis while I was on it. I remember sitting in the doctor's office with my mom and just breaking down in tears after hearing the results of the blood work. I was confused, I was hit with all this bad news, and I was exhausted and still in severe pain.

I found a neurologist during this time who ran several tests and told me I most likely had microscopic nerve damage, but nothing that showed on his testing. He gave me a medication for the nerve pain, which was unbearable. It was always there like fire under my skin. As soon as I set my foot on the floor in the morning, it would run up my legs into my entire body. Both of my Achilles tendons were swollen and tender; the tendons in the front of my legs and into my knees hurt and my arms hurt. This was how I felt every single day. Some days I wondered how I could possibly go on like this. Depression took hold. I just couldn't live like this forever. I couldn't do anything. I couldn't drive, I couldn't go to any of my kids' activities or school events, I didn't see friends, I didn't go out. Period. I was having my groceries delivered and I could barely make food for myself. The house was a bit of a disaster. My husband was working hard and not understanding what was wrong. He had little patience for me trying to figure it out. He just wanted me to "get better." We both wanted that. I was just extremely confused about how.

Back then, I didn't question doctors all that much. They told me what to do and I did it. My neurologist at first was in total agreement with me that my pain was a side effect of Cipro—that is, until he spoke to my rheumatologist. After that he was on board with her thinking it was an autoimmune problem. So now I was on an antidepressant for the nerve pain, a steroid for my overall pain, an anti-inflammatory for my inflamed tendons and physical therapy twice a week.

I found an orthopedist through a Google search. I didn't wait around asking for recommendations. I needed to see someone fast. He was extremely helpful and was one of the very best doctors I had seen. I still recommend him to others to this day. He was very much aware of the side effects of Cipro and had seen other patients with damage. He told me I was actually somewhat lucky. It could have been worse; I could have had tendon ruptures. He also said it was way too much of a coincidence for my pain not to be related to the medications I was on. It didn't make sense for it not to be the side effects. I was so thankful to be understood. He prescribed physical therapy and anti-inflammatories. This was my routine for about a year.

A typical day for me began with waking up exhausted from not sleeping well due to the pain. The less I moved, the better I felt. I would get up and shower, hoping the heat would help in some way. I would then move to the couch, where I would use my heating pad on my arms and legs and alternate it with cold packs. I found the cold numbed the nerve pain. I also had a home TENS machine. A TENS machine is used in physical therapy sessions to stimulate healing. I have no idea if it did me any good, but I continued to use it because I was at a loss as to what else to do. Occasionally I would get a call from a friend checking in. I missed my friends so much. It was heartbreaking to talk to them because it was a reminder of all I was missing. After about a year those calls stopped. Like me, everyone else didn't know what to say or do for me anymore, including my doctors.

Over time my nerve pain started to subside. And when I say time, I mean almost a year. I slowly came off the antidepressant without an increase in my pain, so that was good news. I was so relieved to get off of one medication. Therapy had run its course. I was told "that's all we can do" and "you should be better by now." Is there anything worse to say to someone in pain? These kinds of statements would send me off a cliff of worry and continued to for years until I met some strong women who taught me doctors don't know everything and I needed to take control of my own health. Doctors were sending me on my way, but I wasn't pain free. Far from it. My orthopedist had told me I will likely have chronic pain my entire life from the damage, but I should start exercising as soon as possible. So I slowly started doing gentle workouts again. I began driving once or twice a week. I started to get some sense of normalcy back. Over the next year I stopped therapy and I stopped my anti-inflammatory medications without any increase in my pain. I took Advil to control the pain occasionally. I was on the road to recovery. Or so I thought.

When you experience something like what I went through, it makes you incredibly grateful for all the little things in life you take for granted. And that was certainly the case for me. I had a new appreciation for life. I began working part-time from home, and I began a new exercise routine with the goal of running a 5K. I've never been a runner. I had tried years earlier, but I had always let my back issues stop me. I wanted to try again. My husband bought me a Fitbit for my birthday that year. On the surface this seems like the perfect gift for someone who is active and loves to plan and track everything. I know after reading so much of Gretchen Rubin's work (I dive much deeper into her work in later chapters) that I have a tendency to overdo the rules. For example, if the challenge is to complete ten thousand steps a day, I would go for twelve thousand. I would do crazy things like walk around my bedroom at 9 p.m. getting in more steps. I got carried away and decided I was going to run! Even though I knew in the back of my mind it might inflame my back, I wanted to try.

So I began. I found an app to help me along. And I was loving it. I had a new challenge, which was exciting! But a week or two in I started feeling something was wrong in not only my lower back but also in my neck. I felt a lot of strain in the front of my neck and pain in the back. It was a scary feeling. I was so uncomfortable. I didn't know what was happening. I made an appointment with a doctor at the same orthopedist practice I went to for my tendon and nerve issues. After an MRI, I found out I had two back-to-back herniated discs in my neck and on either side of that, I had two that were degenerative. I also had spinal stenosis, which is when the bulging disc pushes up against the spinal cord. This was the most concerning part. I got no help from this doctor. He gave me a couple of days' worth of muscle relaxers and told me to get a massage! Wow. Really? I was in so much pain and this was his solution? He said if it got worse I was to come back so we could talk about surgery. He also suggested physical therapy. So there I was again, back in therapy. But this time I wasn't getting better; I was getting worse. The pain was actually spreading everywhere. I was so confused. Here I was debilitated again. I was not driving, I was unable to even lie down comfortably, and everything hurt. I was not able to do anything, and I was not getting the right answers from my doctors. I was missing out on life again. I was depressed and anxious. I had thought this part of my life was over, but I was not done.

At this point, I wanted to talk to the orthopedist who helped me so much with my nerve and tendon pain, just to get his opinion because I respected him so much as a doctor. And it was he who sent me to the Spine

7

Institute. He told me that was where he went for his neck issues, the doctors are top-notch, and they avoid surgery if at all possible and use other ways to help their patients feel better. I found out later this is the practice the Washington Redskins use. Finally, a reason to be optimistic. I had a plan.

My first appointment with my new doctor had me feeling I was in good hands, but it also scared me when I realized what I was up against. After seeing my MRI he said, "this is what we see in seventy-year-olds." I was forty-five. "It's not anything you did. The running just accelerated what was going to happen eventually. It's just the genes you were dealt." I was shocked to learn this, but on the other hand I really did relate my pain to the running. It turns out I was just half right. He prescribed a strong anti-inflammatory, along with physical therapy and steroid injections into my neck, all of which I was to start immediately.

The physical therapy center was nothing like where I had been previously. I had one therapist for the entire hour, unlike before, when I'd have multiple people jumping in and out who would then leave me on ice or heat for the last fifteen minutes. I began getting dry needling, exercises and massage at my appointments, which was helping, very, very slowly. But I eventually hit a wall. No more improvement and I was still in pain. I was just beginning to drive again, but not without a lot of discomfort. I tried a massage therapist as well at the same center, and I began one-on-one sessions with a personal trainer there. Both helped a little but did nothing to get me functional again. The personals were costing me a fortune and insurance covered next to nothing. I already had crazy, mounting medical bills and I couldn't stand the stress of adding debt with all of these appointments. And I was still having panic attacks. I had to make a change.

My physical therapist suggested I try one of the group exercise classes offered at the therapy center. I didn't jump on this idea at first because I have never been a "group exercise" type of person. I loved my home workouts. I was fortunate enough to have everything I needed at home (or so I thought) to get my exercise in. I would learn later on that I was not exercising with correct form most of the time, creating more damage to my body. More on this later! I didn't see any benefit to a group class, but I had come to a crossroads. I could see now that the exercises my trainer gave me were helping a little. I just couldn't afford it anymore. So I jumped in, terrified of what was in store for me. But it turns out this was just the beginning of my turning point.

These classes were for people like me with spine issues. The exercises were safe. I walked in, basically shuffling. It hurt to even lie there. I put my body into positions it had not been in for a year or more. Everything was uncomfortable. But the instructor kept me going. She pushed me while at the same time keeping me safe. I continued going three or four times a week. I cried in class. A lot. A simple "How are you today?" would set me off. I was a mess. After a few months I started feeling a change and I was getting better. I started coming to class every day, doing two or three classes a day. I was still anxious. I would still burst into tears occasionally and my trainer would talk me down. One day in a private lesson with her she said to me, "You are strong now. You are trying to exercise your way into feeling better, but the truth is you need to either talk to someone or start meditating." That was a wake-up call. I've been told over the years I should meditate or do something about my anxiety. But I never did. She was telling me if I didn't, things weren't going to change. I didn't understand how reducing my stress was going to help with my overall pain, but I was determined to get my life back completely so I made a decision right there to do whatever I could to get back to normal (or as close as possible) outside of exercise and physical therapy. And that was the beginning of the transformation. The other life-changing piece of advice she gave me came in the form of a book called *Explain Pain* (which I write about in later chapters). I felt like I was reading my own life story. It was eye-opening. I started meditating and following the suggestions in the book, and *that* is when the big changes happened for me.

These classes, my new trainer and the ladies in the group would eventually all become a huge support system for me that would help me finally see real improvement and start my overall "shift" into real wellness, not just physically but also mentally and emotionally. It would be a journey that would lead me down multiple paths with one thing leading to another until I saw the big picture. It would become about so much more than relieving back and neck pain. It would become about making a better life for myself.

The key to all of this was becoming brave, having goals and taking action. I had never before in my life given myself any kind of goals (I am not proud of that, but it's the truth). I now want to share all my growth experiences because I have found them so life changing. I feel like everyone should know how *good* they can feel! I think some of us don't even know how good life can be until we try a few things. It's incredible what we think is "normal," not knowing how much better life *could* be.

Today, I have my life back with almost no limitations. The damage is there, but now I know how to deal with it both mentally and physically, and it will take maintaining both to continue feeling good in my life. As you read through these chapters you will see how I evolved, learned and improved my life way beyond what it was before all of my health problems. I hope to share this story with as many people as possible so they too can learn to have a better life without enduring the pain and suffering I did.

PART 2

HOW IT ALL BEGAN

A Lightening Bolt Moment on the Hallmark Channel

Stay with me here. What does the Hallmark Channel have to do with health and wellness? Well, for me it's where it all began. Years ago when I was dealing with tendon and nerve pain from the prescription drug inter-action, some of the doctors I was seeing remained unconvinced that the side effects of the drugs could be the *only* source of my pain, and they were continuing to do blood tests to check for other causes. I only had one doctor during this time who truly understood because he had seen this reaction in others in his practice. I did not stop seeing the other doctors (for a time) because my blood work showed I actually did have markers for a couple of autoimmune diseases. So I was given more fairly strong drugs to treat these diseases. At the time I knew I had a marker for Sjögren, but now the blood work was showing lupus and rheumatoid arthritis as well. But, logically, with the timing and how it all happened, I knew this was not the cause of my pain and so did my orthopedist. In my search to find someone to help me I saw a chiropractor for a little while who first spoke to me about leaky gut. Even though I ended up leaving that practice to see a surgeon (I have not and did not have any surgeries) regarding my neck and back, my appointments there stayed with me, especially what he said about leaky gut. He explained to me that the Ciproflaxin I was given killed *everything* in my gut and that I would need to heal my gut to help with the pain I was experiencing. He did not explain how this actually happened. I later learned that when we eat inflammatory foods and take anti-inflammatory medications (like Advil), the lining of our gut becomes broken down and leaky, which leads to food particles being released into our bloodstream, which our body then treats as an invader and creates an inflammatory response.

I was sent to yet another practitioner in this practice who explained as best as she could about the foods I could have an intolerance to, not necessarily an allergy to. I was sort of listening. I was so overwhelmed with pain I couldn't really absorb what she was telling me. I didn't think about it again.

A typical day for me during this time was to get up, feel the pain, try to get comfortable, have my mom drive me to my appointments, come home, chat with my mom, have her take care of me, try and get comfortable and go to bed. I was not living at all. Like I said earlier, I wasn't living my life—I was just surviving.

If I watched TV, it was something very low in stress, no news or dramas. The Hallmark Channel was a big favorite with its happy endings and low stress. One day I was watching their morning show and on came this woman, Diane Sanfilippo, cooking and talking about her book, *Practical Paleo*. Suddenly I heard words that sounded familiar: *leaky gut, anti-inflammatory, no sugar*. My ears perked up. This is what the people at the chiropractor's office were trying to explain, but Diane was doing a *much* better job. As soon as the show was over, I grabbed my phone and ordered her book. Within a few days I had finished reading it and made the changes suggested. A lightening bolt moment for sure! It all made perfect sense to me! I changed my diet right then and haven't looked back. That was three years ago.

In a paleo diet for the most part you are to eliminate all processed foods, dairy, sugar, legumes, gluten, grains, soy and unhealthy fats. You then eat whole foods such as vegetables, fruit, meat, seafood, eggs, healthy fats, nuts and seeds. So that's what I did. And did I see a change! Most notably, I had no more stomach pain. I cannot believe how much I tolerated for so long—gas pain, diarrhea (all the time), rashes and acne, and thinking it was just "my normal." No, we can *all* do so much better and live so much better. All of those aliments went away completely when I changed my diet. Also, I wasn't so foggy anymore, which I attribute to eliminating gluten. For many years of my life I was focused on "low fat." Everything I ate had to be low fat. I wouldn't even eat olives in my twenties because I thought they had too much fat! That is a crazy, warped way of thinking about food. But it was the '90s and we were all eating Snackwell's thinking we were doing the right thing. Now that I was eating healthy fat and more protein I was no longer starving and reaching for snacks all day. What a great feeling that was! Wow! Eat and be satisfied! And as for my autoimmune markers, the last time I saw my rheumatologist I was feeling so much better she did not bother checking my levels. She said, "it's more about how you feel than the numbers we see in your blood work." And I stopped the medications she gave me long ago. So I haven't been back in three years. I don't feel the need to. Since my time there I have learned so much about how diet affects autoimmunity.

I'm not here to tell you paleo is the only way to go. But a whole foods diet and eliminating processed foods certainly is. Inflammation is at the root of most chronic diseases. So removing inflammatory foods and foods you have a sensitivity to is extremely important. Have you considered changing your diet? Are you looking to make a change for yourself and/ or your family?

Some of us are Abstainers and some of us are Moderators, according to Gretchen Rubin (Here she is again! I love her work, so I mention her often here). I'm an Abstainer. I can't have "just a little." That would just make it worse. I need to eat it *all* if I have any of whatever it may be.

Abstaining is much easier. Others are Moderators and feel more in control having a little and taking it slow. So think about what would work better for you—jumping right in, or making progressive changes over time. Would you like to make any changes in your diet to improve your overall health? What would those changes be? And why? It's so important to know your why. That's what will keep you on track if you start to struggle with the changes. Keep a Post-it note in your car, on your bathroom mirror, in the kitchen, wherever you will see it to remind yourself the reason you're doing this! My why is I simply don't ever want to deal with the stomach pain, acne and brain fog again. In addition, because of my possible autoimmune issues, eating an anti-inflammatory diet will be a way of life for me so as to never "kick off" those symptoms. Consider the following:

- Decide what changes you would like to make in your diet.

- Commit to eliminating processed foods and eat only real food.

- Know your "why" and place Post-it reminders around your house/car to help keep you on track.

THOUGHTS ON DAIRY

I'm going a little deeper into each part of the paleo diet that had the most effect on me, starting with dairy.

Pretty much my whole life I said I had a "sensitive stomach" or "I have reflux" when the truth was a simple diet change corrected these issues for me. I don't know why the doctors I saw over the years never suggested I may have lactose intolerance. Until I simply tried cutting it out myself I didn't know either (a lesson in taking control right there).

My acid levels were also all out of whack. It's amazing to me now that I can eat anything I want without any heartburn at all. I was someone who was on Nexium and still having issues. Not just cutting dairy, but my overall paleo diet corrected all of this for me. And no more over-the-counter medication, which is even better. Looking back, I can see now that a multitude of symptoms were coming from my consumption of dairy. Random rashes, stomach pain and gas, diarrhea, acne and allergies. I just do not get acne anymore. At all. Period. And my seasonal allergies are much, much less severe. Noticeably so. No more sinus infections or asthma. Such a better quality of life! How many people just live with being this uncomfortable and try taking over-the-counter medications that don't really do the job? Too many is my guess.

You might be thinking *I can't give up cheese!* Well, you may not have any issues with dairy and that's fine. Take a look at the quality of the food you are consuming. Is it grass fed? Is it whole milk? Is it organic? I also suggest whole milk vs. 1 percent, 2 percent or fat-free milk. These products are highly processed and stripped of all healthy fats. Healing a leaky gut is so important to our overall health and preventing chronic disease! How would you feel if you gave it a shot for thirty days, just to see what would happen? No harm there.

I still enjoy ghee, which is a clarified butter. I'm getting all the benefits of the healthy fats without the lactose. Alternatives for cream and milk include full-fat coconut milk. The cream on top of the can is an excellent replacement for cream used in soups, sauces, etc. Many people who can't eat products with cow's milk do just fine with goat's milk. I will occasionally have a little goat cheese without any issues. Everyone is different! The key is to know your body and what works for you. So think about eliminating dairy from your diet if you have any symptoms you think could stem from dairy. Try the following.

- Eliminate all forms of dairy for thirty days.

- Replace butter with ghee.

- Replace cream and milk with coconut milk or other nut milks (e.g., almond).

- After thirty days reassess. How are you feeling? What's different?

DITCHING THE SUGAR

We all know sugar is not good for you. But do you know how bad is actually is? I didn't. I grew up hearing sugar rots your teeth and makes you fat. And although that is certainly true, it does so much more. Sugar causes inflammation among other things, which in turn causes a multitude of chronic diseases. Read more here: https://www.rd.com/health/wellness/what-sugar-does-to-your-body/.

You can read about the link between sugar and cancer here: https://www.cnn.com/2019/07/10/health/sugary-drinks-cancer-risk-study-intl/index.html

Sugar was fairly easy for me to give up for a couple of reasons.

- There are *so* many alternatives to processed sugar.
- Once I knew what it was doing to my body, I was completely on board.

That is partially my personality type at work (I'm an Upholder—see *The Four Tendencies* by Gretchen Rubin: https://gretchenrubin.com/books/the-four-tendencies/intro/). Once I decide to do something, I'm all in.

I think the best alternative to processed sugar is honey and organic pure maple syrup. I bake and cook with both. When I first eliminated sugar I was baking a lot of paleo recipes to fend off my sugar cravings. But now I do that only maybe once a month or so. If I want something sweet I eat fruit or a Lärabar®. My taste buds have completely changed.

Processed food is not food. Period. It's what some of us have become accustomed to, to the detriment of our health. Sugar is hiding in things you may not think of. We all know it's in sodas, desserts and the obvious places, but you will also find it in bottled salad dressings, condiments, soups, etc. A lot of foods labeled as organic still have sugar. Reading labels is key. Pretty much anything in a box or a can has sugar with few exceptions. Some companies are coming around due to demand, but it's slow. I was raised making our family recipe for salad dressing since I was a kid, so I'm not one to buy bottled dressings, but if you haven't tried making your own, I promise it's super simple. Or just throw some oil and vinegar/salt and pepper on your salad. And yes, I do like cooking. That also makes it easier. But I think cooking is a life skill! Not some chore to complain about like cleaning a bathroom. Your health is the number one most important thing. Without it you have nothing. I know this to be true firsthand. Until you lose it maybe you're not aware of how important it is and how important what you eat is to your health. No dessert will ever be that enticing to me when I look at it this way. I feel good. And that's all I need. And I want to stay that way.

Have you thought about eliminating sugar from your diet? Try the following steps. Remember, it's good to know your personality type. It will help you figure out the best approach for your internal expectations. I highly suggest taking Gretchen Rubin's quiz here: https://quiz.gretchenrubin.com/. Once you know your personality type, everything you want to do for yourself becomes easier!

- Decide to eliminate sugar from your diet.

- Shop! Read the labels. Pay attention. Avoid sugar, corn syrup, fructose, etc. Buy replacements like honey and maple syrup.

- Try a few recipes for baked goods, salad dressings and replacements for your favorite foods. I suggest recipes by Cassie Joy Garcia and Diane Sanfilippo, or any quick Google search for paleo recipes will do the trick.

- If you are having a craving, eat fruit.

- When eating out, just ask! Be *that* person. Ha! I am. I ask, I alter, whatever I need to do to get what I want. I've never had a restaurant not comply.

TO BEAN OR NOT TO BEAN

Okay, that was corny I know. But it made me giggle. Let's discuss legumes. Legumes are one of those foods that have a reputation for being part of a healthy diet for their fiber and protein content. But they also have lectins that irritate the lining of your gut, which leads to leaky gut and can be a problem for those of us with autoimmune issues. Read more about how lectins affect the body here: https://www.health.usnews.com.

But what about the people of the Blue Zones who make beans part of their regular diet? The people of the Blue Zones are the people in the world with the longest life expectancy as studied by National Geographic. Many, many factors play into that longevity, and you can read more about it here: https://www.ncbi.nlm.nih.gov/pmc/articles/PMC6125071/.

With my autoimmune markers I choose not to eat beans. They obviously cause gut irritation and gas, and I try to keep my gut as healthy as possible. There is a lot of hype about the fiber and protein beans have, but you can get that and more from some vegetables, like broccoli and Brussels sprouts. My goal is to not eat anything that will disrupt my microbiome, especially because I'm still taking an anti-inflammatory for my neck and back issues. I am currently testing the waters of getting off them completely. That is my goal because anti-inflammatory medications also destroy the lining of your gut. So I'm super vigilant about my food because I'm still taking this medication. That said, it is *not* as powerful of a drug as I was on in the beginning. I'm now taking Meloxicam, which is a generic for Mobic. I will get there. Right now I skip a pill here and there without any issue. My doctor seems to think I will feel more pain if I go off of it, but I'm not convinced of that. I know my body. (As of the writing of this book, I'm off of my daily anti-inflammatory. I now take it only on an as-needed basis.) What is left for me to deal with is more muscular that anything else, and yoga is working that out for me. I'm getting way ahead of myself here! More on all of that later! I got off topic a bit, but my point is, I'm choosing to stay away from anything that would cause leaky gut or any other health problems for my own mental and physical well-being.

Did you know peanuts are legumes also? I didn't until a few years ago. This is one of the reasons why my blog is called *My Awakened Well-Being*! I was asleep at the wheel of my health for *so long*. There was so much I didn't know or didn't pay attention to. I noticed a few years ago that I did not feel well after eating peanut butter or peanuts. And not in an "allergic" way: an upset stomach, a tight throat—all around not good. Peanuts are not nuts; they are part of the legume family. So this makes complete sense to me. I now eat cashew butter and almond butter instead. Try dipping apple slices into almond butter. It's my go-to snack! Sometimes I roll up a grain-free tortilla with organic fruit preserves and cashew butter. My version of PB and J! So good! What are your thoughts on legumes? Are they a regular part of your diet? Try the following:

- Pay attention to how you feel after eating legumes. Do you have stomach pain, gas, bloating?

- Go a week without legumes and up your high protein and fiber vegetable intake.

- Assess how you feel without legumes.

One more thing! I'd like to provide you with a link to *The Four Tendencies* by Gretchen Rubin for those who are interested. I write a lot about her and her work on my blog because I find it so incredibly useful. If you want to go deeper or if you haven't taken the quiz, you may want to read the book for insights into your own personality. Enjoy! https://www. amazon.com/gp/product/1524760919/ref=as_li_tl?ie=UTF8&tag=my-awakenedwel-20&camp=1789&creative=9325&linkCode=as2&cre-ativeASIN=1524760919&linkId=961771dc8819af9694a02c2b808778c7

ALL OILS ARE NOT CREATED EQUAL

Do you know the story of how we as a culture started eating things like vegetable oils? I was fairly shocked to learn these oils were used in manufacturing until someone had the brilliant idea of selling them as a replacement for lard in this country. And so began the uptick in heart attacks in the US population. This article explains it very well. I think it's a must read and an extremely eye-opening look at how we got to this point. I really hope you take a minute to read it: https://www.theatlantic.com/health/archive/2012/04/how-vegetable-oils-replaced-animal-fats-in-the-american-diet/256155/.

Eating only healthy oils is another part of the paleo diet I adhere to. This means I stick to olive oil, coconut oil and ghee. Unfortunately for me, avocado oil is out. Avocados give me horrendous stomach pain. It's disappointing because so many healthy alternative foods and recipes are made with avocado oil! If you don't have a sensitivity to avocados, by all means include it in your diet! In the end it doesn't stop me from enjoying everything I want.

Knowledge is power. Know what you are eating. We have been told not to eat animal fat, but instead eat these vegetable oils that cause heart disease. Animal fats are not the enemy. I avoid eating anything with canola oil, safflower oil, vegetable oil, etc. Take a look at some food labels around your house. Vegetable oils are in everything. Are you baking with canola oil? Is it in your salad dressing? It's most likely in any chips or processed foods you have. My thought is, why would I eat something I know will cause my body harm when alternatives are out there? I still eat chips but now only the ones made with olive oil. They are out there. You can find them on Amazon and at Whole Foods and Trader Joe's among other places. It's even easier to find them made with avocado oil! I bake and cook with coconut oil, olive oil and ghee. It's really a simple replacement.

It's all about choices and your "why." Why am I eating this way? Why do I want to change? That's what motivates you and will keep you on track! Would you like to make the change to eating healthier oils? Try the following.

- Go through your pantry and refrigerator/freezer, read the labels and toss anything with the following oils: vegetable, safflower, sunflower, soybean, canola, rapeseed, corn and peanut.

- Replace vegetable oils with olive oil, avocado oil, coconut oil or ghee.

- Use these oils when cooking and baking! Feel good about your choices!

- When eating out, just *ask*. If your server doesn't know, they can and most likely will find out for you.

MY FOGGY BRAIN

I dabbled in being gluten free when I was seeing the chiropractor who first suggested to me I may have leaky gut. But I was floundering trying to do it myself. I was clueless. I got rid of things, but didn't have any replacements. I didn't know what to eat or how to cook. Needless to say that didn't last long. In fact, I didn't do it long enough then to feel any changes. Fast-forward to when I discovered *Practical Paleo* by Diane Sanfilippo, and I had an actual plan as to how to cut gluten out and how to use other flours such as cassava and coconut in my baking and cooking. I just needed guidance, and her book was like my Bible. I still refer to it again and again. It covers everything!

You may have heard gluten can cause brain fog. That was absolutely true for me, but, again, how do you know at the time gluten is what is causing the problem without actually trying to eliminate it? I just thought *Wow, isn't it weird how I sometimes can't find the words to say?* Or I would hear myself talking slowly, as though talking took a lot of effort. That is not normal, and certainly not normal for the old or new me. You just don't know how good you can feel until you take gluten out of your diet. Also with all the gastrointestinal problems gluten causes in those who are sensitive to it, it is difficult to say how much of my distress was due to gluten and how much was due to lactose. I've accidentally had dairy when eating out and I most definitely felt it! Other times eating out I knew there was no dairy yet it still upset my stomach, so I would guess that was gluten. These things occasionally happen when eating out. The restaurants are always accommodating to the best of their ability, but sometimes they just don't know exactly what is in the food, depending on the type of restaurant and how knowledgeable the staff is. Some people reintroduce the foods eliminated in the paleo diet to see how they do and what they can tolerate. Diane gives a wonderful explanation on how to do this in her book. But with my autoimmune issues, I have no interest in reintroducing anything into my diet that I've taken out.

There are some conflicting opinions out there about gluten. Some say you don't need to avoid it unless you have celiac disease. But new research is showing you can still be sensitive to gluten without having celiac disease. Doctors are starting to listen to their patients. Gluten is another culprit in destroying the lining of our stomachs. It's actually the way gluten is processed in food that causes it to give us trouble. You can read more about that here: https://www.webmd.com/digestive-disorders/celiac-disease/features/gluten-intolerance-against-grain#2.

If you are considering eliminating gluten from your diet, try the following:

- Remove all gluten products from your pantry. Remove all flours and grains, including corn meal, rice, wheat and white flour.

- Replace the flours and grains with cassava flour, coconut flour and tapioca flour.

- Do a search for gluten-free or, better yet, paleo versions of your favorite recipes. I always suggest *Practical Paleo* to start!

- Evaluate how you feel. What's different? Do you have less brain fog? Is your stomach feeling better?

ADDING THE GOOD STUFF

I've written a lot about what I eliminated from my diet—now I want to write about what I've added. I'm fast-forwarding a bit to when I was earning my holistic health coaching certification, which I did because I was desperate to know more. I'm so passionate on the subject of holistic health these days. I can't get enough information. I'm in constant learning mode. A couple of books I read in my studies that made the most impact on my diet were *How Not to Die* by Michael Greger, MD, FACLM, and *The Whole Foods Diet* by John Mackey, Alona Pulde, MD, and Matthew Lederman, MD. The glaring message I got was I was *not* incorporating enough variety of vegetables into my diet, among other things. And I was not aware of the power some of these vegetables hold. That food is medicine has never been so clear. For example, the broccoli family of cruciferous vegetables are just powerhouses themselves. In addition to broccoli, radishes, cabbage, collard greens, Brussels sprouts, cauliflower, artichokes, arugula and kale are all part of the cruciferous family. As stated in *The Whole Foods Diet*, "Not only are these diverse foods all related, they also share extraordinary health benefits, particularly for preventing cancer." Dr. Joel Fuhrman points out that cruciferous vegetables are the most micronutrient dense of all vegetables and calls them "the most powerful anticancer foods in existence."

There isn't a vegetable I don't like, but I can tell you I was not eating enough vegetables in this category. A simple change was to add kale to every salad. Sometimes kale is enough; other times I get another green to fix with it. I also add broccoli sprouts to almost every salad I make! I shoot for eating one or two vegetables from this family every day.

Flaxseed is another powerful food that was totally off my radar. Read more about the benefits of flaxseed here: https://www.webmd.com/diet/

features/benefits-of-flaxseed#1. This is another salad staple. Why wouldn't I add it?

As my diet stands right now, my priorities are high-quality proteins, a large variety of fruits and vegetables at *every meal*, seeds and nuts and healthy oils. If you want to hear an incredible story of how food truly is medicine, I highly recommend you read about Dr. Terry Wahls, MD. She beat her progressive multiple sclerosis (MS) with diet and functional medicine. These stories are out there. Why don't we hear them more? No money to be made in food as medicine is my guess. It is *so* important to understand how much we can help ourselves with the help of functional medicine doctors and our diets. To read more about Dr. Wahls, click here: https://terrywahls.com/about/about-terry-wahls/. Are you looking to add more variety to your diet? Try the following:

- Shop for raw nuts (remember peanuts are not nuts!) Raw is best, but if you buy roasted, look out for nuts with peanut oil and other unhealthy oils. Trader Joe's and Aldi are my favorite places to find healthy nuts.

- Incorporate more vegetables into your diet, and especially look to add cruciferous ones whenever you can. Try cauliflower rice, steamed broccoli, cabbage and kale in salads and roasted Brussels sprouts. They are all delicious!

PART 3

SELF KNOWLEDGE AND IMPROVEMENT

Starting to Find Myself and My Tribe

My first day of exercise class at my therapy center went like this. I walked toward the room and was met by another lady, beautiful, older than me, but very elegant. She asked if it was my first class and what my issues were (because you would not be exercising there if you *did not* have issues of some kind). As soon as I began to explain my story the tears started. I was so drained at this point. I had been in physical therapy for more than a year. I *had* made progress. I was driving myself to class—that alone was huge. But the pain was still everywhere and unbearable. I had tried one-on-one training, but looking back now, I can see I wasn't ready for that. This class was my last shot. Everyone in the class at that time was older than me. But as I joked, my doctor said I have the spine of a seventy-year-old, so I fit right in. Everyone was very warm; the trainer was full of energy. She was ten years younger than me and easily the strongest woman I have ever met.

These women were readers, volunteers, teachers, world travelers, mothers and grandmothers. They had similar interests to mine like going to the ballet, museum exhibits, art shows and concerts. And later on more women my age joined and they also were interesting people. We all became close. We understood each other's struggles. But these women were different from my other friends in that there were no taboo subjects. We just talked openly and honestly about everything. From news headlines, to family issues, religion, you name it. No one held back and it was fantastic. I loved these women! It's freeing to have uncensored conversations and no worry about offending someone. If you disagree, you move on. There's no hiding or not speaking your mind. I loved it. And it made me realize I hadn't had these kinds of people in my life before. I was curating my tribe before I knew I needed to. That would come later when I started really working on myself. I'm not blaming anyone. I would hold back. I have *a lot* to say and I'm a highly emotional person. And that's not a bad thing, unless you feel like the minority all the time. I wasn't with the right people. I think as moms we don't always choose our own friends. At least this was true for me. I hung out with my kids' friends' parents for years and years. And I truly liked most of them. We would get drinks, go to lunch, etc. But were these my people? No. It was superficial. I was superficial. A lot was missing. It took me needing *real* friendship and these women showing up in my life at just the right time. I was so beaten down and fragile at this point. Just one of them asking "How are you today?" would send me into tears. My life was not normal at that point, and they understood that better than anyone else did and they actually listened. I needed that so badly.

By the end of the first year I was feeling much better. I was doing more on my own. I was starting to go out to enjoy things again, but I still had quite a lot of pain. In later chapters I write about the incredible insights my trainer Carrie had regarding my wellness. She has now established herself in her own personal training business, Transformative Training, bringing her amazing talents to more people in need of her help.

Look at your own exercise routine. First, are you exercising at all? Do you feel like you are using correct form in what you are doing? Are you exercising alone? Do you want the support of a group? Try the following:

- If exercise is new to you, try walking just a few minutes a day to start and then add on a little more time every day.

- Try working with a personal trainer even just one time to have them look at everything you are doing. It's important to have those eyes on you to prevent injury.

- Take a group class of some sort. There is *so much* out there! And it doesn't need to be expensive. Look at your local recreation centers. Locally I can pay six dollars for a day of whatever classes I want and access to all the machines. Quite a deal. Just make sure you like the instructor and they are watching for good form. Not all instructors are created equal. I promise the boost you will get from the people in the group is priceless. And if you don't get a boost, those aren't your people. Keep trying different groups until you hit on the one.

THE BOOK THAT CHANGED EVERYTHING

A few years ago, when I was still in the throes of my recovery, my personal trainer Carrie suggested I read a book called *Explain Pain* by David Butler and Lorimer Moseley. I was at a point where I had gained strength and had continued physical therapy, but continued to have significant pain that would send me off emotionally and also keep me from doing more of what I loved to do. Everyone had their theories as to what was going on, but the only person in my life who was up front and honest with me was Carrie. She basically told me I couldn't fix the pain I was feeling with exercise. She was saying it was in my head, which was true, but not (I explain this later). It was *real* alright, and she knew it. She also told me I needed to start meditating or go talk to someone. She was telling me I needed a different kind of therapy.

This conversation I had with Carrie was extremely emotional for me. No one had spoken to me this way before about my anxiety. Ever, in my entire life. She was brutally honest. It was jarring to hear her words spoken directly to me like that and I was a bit shocked. I sat there in tears. It felt like some sort of emotional breakthrough. I am *forever* grateful for her for being this honest with me, for seeing I needed to hear these things in a way that would wake me up. No one in my family would have ever talked to me this way, and if they had I probably would have been so angry with them I wouldn't have listened anyway. The fact that it came from someone on the outside meant I could no longer hide that part of myself. It was obvious to her and she did the right thing by making me confront it.

Two things she suggested were *Explain Pain* and a meditation app called Insight Timer (which I now use every day religiously, starting the day after she suggested it). As soon as I began reading *Explain Pain* I was taken with it immediately. I was reading my story. I couldn't believe it! Finally I could see myself in the pages and I started to understand. Right from page two it became clear. "When pain persists and feels like it is ruining your life, it is difficult to see how it can serve any useful purpose. But even when pain is chronic and nasty, it hurts because the brain has concluded, for some reason or another, that you are threatened and in danger and need protecting—the trick is finding out why the brain has come to this conclusion." Clearly, I needed to figure out how to get over my fear of pain. It was time to take control and work out the threats or feel like this forever. I made a decision right then that I will do whatever suggested to reverse what had happened to me.

I also learned stress can make nerve pain worse and damaged nerves become sensitive to the chemicals you produce when you are stressed. This made perfect sense to me because of the unbelievable stress and worry I was having at the time when my pain was spreading and getting worse and no one could tell me why. The authors also explained that "things that used to hurt, now hurt more. And things that didn't hurt before, now hurt." There I was, right there on the page. This was exactly what I had experienced. And for the first time there was an explanation. I was so relieved to see my story in print. Someone gets it! Other identifying statements I read were "It started off so simply and now it has spread" and "No one seems to believe me." I basically said those exact words. Something else that really hit home for me was that even the *fear* or *anticipation* of pain may be enough to prevent changes from returning to normal. Returning to normal was all I wanted. Clearly, I needed to figure out how to get over my fear of pain.

Now I had my goals and was motivated to get started. With the understanding that the pain was coming from my brain, not the tissue/nerve damage, I now knew what I needed to work on to get my life back to as normal as possible.

Are you dealing with chronic pain? Do you have fears of certain movements, reinjuring yourself or making it worse? Fears of botched surgery? Or other fears? I want to give you a few action steps to apply to your own life if you feel like this speaks to your situation. You could:

- Decide to take control and work out the threats. Just deciding to do this is a *huge* step.

- Have a goal. What is it you want to do more of without pain? Walking, reading, driving, playing with your kids? You decide. But I suggest picking one to start and focusing on that.

- Increase activity with slow exposure.

This seems simple enough, but honestly it's a *big* decision, and it takes strength to move forward. You can do this!

EXPLAIN PAIN PART 2

Once I finished reading *Explain Pain* and saw my story in those pages, I decided I *must* do what it takes to correct this or I will never feel the way I want to. I needed to change my mindset and retrain my brain immediately. Four things were clear from my reading:

- Work out the threats.

- Take control.

- Have goals.

- Work on mindfulness and coping skills.

Let's start with working out the threats. According to the authors, "Fear or anticipation of pain may be enough to prevent changes in returning to normal." Well, at that time I most certainly had fears over many things and I was avoiding them like the plague. Here is a list of some of the fears listed in the book that were spot on for me:

- The seriousness of my situation.

- Pain.

- Not knowing.

- Certain movements.

- Making it worse.

- Not being able to work.

- Not being able to look after my parents.

So in addition to my daily pain I was constantly thinking and worrying about all of the above. This made my brain think I was under threat all the time, which just increased the pain. It's a truly vicious cycle. To avoid that cycle I needed to do the following:

- Be brave.

- Have understanding.

- Confront my fears.

Which is what I set out to do. And still do! Most recently I tried a new exercise class. This falls under the "making it worse" category. I used to get so worked up over new movements. For example, after about one year of exercise classes at my therapy center, Carrie added a sculpt class using kettlebells. I wanted to do it, but fear took over. I said, "I can't do that. My back and neck will hurt." Carrie told me to come to class and do the exercises without the kettlebells in order to get used to the movement and get over my fear. And that actually worked. Once I did pick up the weights, there were many tears. I would stand in class holding my kettlebell with tears of fear coming down my face. But I did it. Over and over again. Until my brain realized there was no threat and I realized I wasn't going to hurt myself. The trick is mental. Let me be clear—I *did* feel worse initially. But, as Carrie explained to me, this was because I was doing something "new" and my body had to get used to it. It took a long time, but she was right. I thank God she came into my life! No doctor or physical therapist had ever explained this to me before and it was exactly what I needed to hear! The combination of reading *Explain Pain* then practicing it in class was magical. It was like therapy, not for my body, but for my mind. I was truly retraining my brain. I could see it working. And I saw it a year or so later when I started yoga as well, or anytime I do something new. Remember it's new and it's okay. Feel the fear and do it anyway.

Next was taking control. For the longest time I would go from doctor to physical therapist to massage therapist to my trainer and would be sent down a hundred different roads. They would contradict each other in their advice. It was incredibly confusing. At some point I had to take control of the situation and listen to my body. I grew up believing doctors know everything. I did exactly what they told me to the letter (Upholder behavior again). I never questioned them, ever. This is one of those not so great traits of being an Upholder. I should have asked more questions of those helping me. I should have made my own decisions about my care *earlier* instead of sitting around waiting for one of them to magically cure me.

Again it was Carrie who started me thinking differently. She was not only physically strong but also mentally strong, and she built me up to be confident in myself and my decision-making to a point I never had before. Just one practitioner saying to me "I don't know why you are feeling that way" or "I don't know why you aren't getting better" would send me off the deep end of worry. I don't do that anymore. I'm in control. I realize practitioners don't know everything. They are making their best guess, but ultimately I am in charge of my body and health. This is so freeing! I no longer am fearful of doctors! I don't look at them like they are the be all end all as I used to. I listen, I think it through, *then* I act.

Moving on to having goals. There's a concept! Did you grow up having goals? I didn't. Never of any kind whatsoever. Not academically, not personally, not financially. I didn't understand how life changing having goals can be. Having goals is how we move through life and get what we want. Otherwise everything just happens to you. That's how I lived the first forty-four years of my life. So I made small goals to start (this is a huge focus for me later on). For now, my first goal was to take short walks without flare-ups to my back or neck. I started with three minutes. That's it. Then I added a minute or two until I worked my way up. I now do regular walks of thirty to forty minutes without a problem. I recently walked all day in New York City and I did have a flare-up, but it was gone after two days. And to me that is still a win.

The fourth concept was becoming mindful and learning coping skills—two more things I never had done. Carrie asked me if I had ever meditated, and I said I had not, but I'd been told many times over the years that I should meditate or "do something about your anxiety." I never did until having this conversation one-on-one with someone I completely trusted and knew was in my corner 100 percent. I did a quick Google search and found the following article that I printed, cut and pasted into my new wellness notebook I had started when I started my private sessions with Carrie. Little did I know what this notebook would be become over the next two years.

I found "Strategies for Good Mental Health Wellness." The following are coping skills suggested in dealing with stressful situations.

- Build confidence.

- Make time for family and friends.

- Give and accept support.

- Create a meaningful budget.

- Volunteer.

- Manage stress.

- Find strength in numbers.

- Identify and deal with moods.

- Learn to be at peace with yourself.

I had *so much* to work on here. All but accept compliments and find strength in numbers were areas that needed *vast* improvement. One more list I found on coping skills was extremely helpful. Here we go:

- Problem-solve.

- Remember it's your life.

- Be proud of surviving.

- Develop insight.

- Use humor.

- Be realistic, not dramatic.

- Get support.

- Don't look for blame.

- Do something.

Whoa. This list had some big ahas for me—most definitely problem-solving, be realistic, not dramatic, develop insight and *do something*. Yes, this was an important list too. And a lot of these skills I would work on after reading yet another book, but I get to that later. I read *Explain Pain*, I found out what I needed to do to fix what was happening to me and now I had a jumping-off point.

When I look at my notebook from this time in my life it's like looking at another person as I read what I wrote. But I also see how clear it is that

I am where I am today because of it. Here are my first notes and goals I gave myself.

- Find volunteer opportunities.

- Spend more time with parents.

- Rekindle friendships/make lunch dates.

- Daily gratitude practice.

- Focus on problem-solving.

- Find humor in my situation.

- Read every day.

- Meditate every day.

- Maybe get back into gardening and cooking.

- Consider doing another Happiness Project.

All roads lead to Gretchen Rubin! I had done a Happiness Project probably eight or so years earlier. I thought I would do another because this would be the time. This was the beginning. It would be my starting point of everything that would change my life in the next two years. I'm always working on myself. As I sit here typing I occasionally think *Is this going to hurt my neck?* I'm still fighting the "making it worse" threat. The difference now is that I think it, but I do it anyway and guess what? I'm fine. Maybe a little stiff, but fine. In my next few pages I write about how I did my Happiness Project and the next book that helped me through this time of learning and healing. Think about your own situation and try the following:

- Read through the coping skills listed earlier and decide which, if any, you would like to or need to work on.

- List goals and ideas to get you there.

- Break those down into smaller steps you can do every day to reach your goals!

LEARNING MY ABCDE'S

In addition to *Explain Pain*, Carrie recommended I read *Learned Optimism: How to Change Your Mind and Your Life* by Martin E. P. Seligman, PhD. This was my introduction to positive psychology, a fairly new science. By definition, positive psychology is "the scientific study of what makes life most worth living" or "the scientific study of positive human functioning and flourishing on multiple levels that include the biological, personal, relational, institutional, cultural and global dimensions of life." I was about to take another big step in my healing and growing with the help of this book.

The biggest takeaway for me was learning to dispute my own beliefs and become skilled at generating alternatives. This was really important to understand given that I was afraid to do half the things that would help me get stronger and heal for fear of hurting myself. *Explain Pain* says the fear of pain can prevent change, so I had to overcome my fears. I also had to de-catastrophize. My beliefs and thoughts were stopping me from doing a lot of basic things. As I was focusing on my diet, physical therapy and exercise, I cut out every doctor from my life at that time with the exception of those at the Spine Institute. I just could not handle another piece of bad news. If I didn't go to the doctor, no bad news. This was my thinking. I didn't even go to the dentist for fear the dental chair would hurt my neck. Also I had a general fear of doctors because their negligence in giving me a drug combination that injured me was still at the forefront of my mind. So much fear. It was paralyzing. So I had my fears in movements and activities and I had a fear of learning anymore about my health for the sake of not going off the deep end completely. I didn't get a checkup, a dental cleaning, a pap smear or a flu shot for four years. Yes, four years. That's a long time.

What helped me start to make the change was a strategy I found in *Learned Optimism* called the ABCDE model. The ABCDE stands for Adversity (what happened), Belief (how you interpret the adversity), Consequences (feelings and what you did), Disputation (argue and dispute your beliefs) and Energization (outcome or effects from redirecting your thoughts).

Here is my first attempt at using the ABCDE Model to dispute my fears. I started with what was most pressing at the moment. Remember when I said I started my sculpt class with no weights? I also decided for myself that deadlifts weren't good for me and my back because the first time I did them I had pain. This pain eventually faded, but it was enough to scare me. My first ABCDE episode would be about this conclusion I made up for myself. It looked like this:

A (Adversity)	Do a deadlift in class with weight.
B (Belief)	I will hurt my back.
C (Consequence)	I feel afraid and frustrated.
D (Disputation)	Carrie is very skilled and would not put me in danger.
E (Energization)	I tried it, had some pain, then it faded.

For the record, I do deadlifts with kettlebells on a regular basis now with no pain. Two things happened. I got over my fear and my body got used to a new movement. It takes time. A long time. I had to be patient. I felt a little pain with deadlifts for a while, but guess what? That doesn't happen anymore!

Here's another I did shortly after regarding my fear of getting a flu shot.

A (Adversity)	I am afraid to get a flu shot.
B (Belief)	Something will go wrong and I will have a reaction to the shot or my body won't take it well.
C (Consequence	I am scared and procrastinating.
D (Disputation)	I have had flu shots in the past and been fine. Everyone in my family has had shots this year and they are all fine

E (Energization)	My son and I got our flu shots together. This way I had someone with me and I had to be the "grown up" and not freak out. Having him there kept me calm even though he had no idea he was doing that for me. I didn't have any kind of reaction.

In my notebook next to where I wrote this is a little side note that says, "I did it! 10/20/18." Small steps. It was clear I needed to use this model and learn how to find the evidence against my beliefs and show the flaws. According to the author, the facts will be on my side most of the time. I don't know exactly when I became so pessimistic in my thinking. Maybe the turmoil I had gone through left me that way. Seligman explains that "pessimistic thinking consists of latching onto the most dire possible belief, not because the evidence supports it, but precisely because it is so dire." This was key for me. Over the next few years I continued to use this strategy to catch up on my health checkups. I finally went to the dentist, I got my pap smear, and last I went to my internist, the one I dreaded the most and had the most fear about seeing. Turns out I had a clean bill of health at all of these appointments! Okay, I had one cavity. Four years without a cleaning will do that to you. Do you struggle with negative thinking? Try the following: in your daily life over the next week tune into any adversity that comes along. Listen to your thoughts. When you hear negative thoughts, dispute them! And record them using the ABCDE model.

MY HAPPINESS PROJECT ROUND 2

Previously, I wrote about strategies for maintaining good mental health. One of them was to learn to be at peace with yourself. That really caught my attention and was very different from the other strategies. "Get to know who you are, what makes you really happy and learn to balance what you can and cannot change about yourself." This was an aha moment for me. Out of nowhere I remembered that eight years earlier I had done a Happiness Project after reading Gretchen Rubin's book *The Happiness Project*. I had completely forgotten about this book until this moment. I ran to my bookshelf for it and there it was, just waiting for me. The goal of *The Happiness Project* is the same as the strategy I was working on. Get to know who you are and what makes you happy! The other side of that is to stop all the things other people find fun and you don't. One of the big lessons of that book was that just because someone else finds something fun doesn't mean I have to. I don't let people talk me into things I know I won't enjoy. That doesn't mean I don't try new things. I just am way more in touch with myself. I know now what I consider fun and, honestly, I've always known, but now I'm being authentic. I love going to concerts and music in general. I love reading, cooking, planning, hot sunny weather, fitness and exercise, going to museums and the arts in general. There's more, but those are the big ones. Not everyone will find those things fun, and that's okay. It's all about knowing what makes you happy and doing that.

Years ago, when *The Happiness Project* was first published, I jumped right in. I was thirty-nine years old, loved the book and thought *That looks fun*. Fast-forward to 2017. I'm forty-seven years old and a mess and looking at another Happiness Project for completely different reasons. So this strategy of learning to be at peace with yourself struck a cord immediately. In my wellness notebook I wrote next to it: "Consider doing another Happiness Project?" And that's what I did.

If you are unfamiliar with the book, I suggest giving it a read whether you choose to do the project or not. Basically once you come up with your resolutions, you choose a quote to keep you motivated and then break the resolution down into actions you will do daily or weekly, for the entire month. My first resolution, which I started in November 2017 (again, so thankful for my journaling) looked like this:

This Month's Resolution: Conquer Fears (Take Control)

My quotation: "Don't let your fear of what could happen make nothing happen."

Daily/Weekly Actions
Take timed walks.
Progress with different shoes.
Take timed baths.
Visualize.
Refute fears in writing (see ABCDE model).
Get back on my computer.

Taking timed walks and refuting my fears in writing I've addressed already. So you know where I was headed on those resolutions. Let's talk about the shoes! Ah, the shoes! I only wore *one* pair for at least a year and a half. I'm sure you can guess why! Fear that any other shoes would hurt my back! I couldn't even wear what you would call regular athletic shoes. All the technology going on in the bed of the shoes would throw my neck out of whack. I still don't wear them. I'll admit I'm not wearing heels (yet!), but I wear whatever flats I want. This may seem small and trivial to you, but to me it was a *real* fear. I was afraid of more pain. Period. So retraining my brain was the goal.

The same went for taking baths, another activity that hurt my back and neck. I can't explain it. So many small things were really big things. Remember what *Explain Pain* said: progress slowly with timed activities until your body and brain realize there is no threat. I take baths now without any problem. This was not a fun one. It was really uncomfortable at first. I had to be willing to deal with being uncomfortable to get to the good stuff. I don't linger in there for hours like I used to with a book and a glass of wine, but I still get to enjoy it and that's all that matters.

Visualization is amazing. Did you know your brain doesn't know if you are actually doing the thing you are visualizing or not? It's a *great* way to conquer fears! So I would regularly visualize myself doing all the things

I was afraid of doing. Walking, wearing different shoes, sitting in the bath, all without pain. I still do this on a regular basis for whatever may have me rattled or whatever I want my future self to be doing. I plan to get deeper into this in the future as I feel like I could get even more out of it.

Getting back on my computer was a big one. It just sat on my bedroom desk like this big scary thing. I missed it. I was still totally connected to the world because of my phone, but sitting at the computer brought immediate neck tension. So, like I did with everything else at that time, I avoided it to the point that I was then afraid of it. I started ever so slowly. I'd write one email, look up one thing, spending a few minutes at a time on the computer. It took a very long time to get over this one. And for my own sake, I still don't stay on for hours on end. No one should, really—it's not the best for anyone's neck and back! When I decided to get certified as a holistic health coach, I realized I would be on the computer quite a bit. I thought *It's school. It will be required.* And I dove in. I'm glad I had progressed slowly. I now make sure I have really good posture when working on the computer. Better than ever before. When I see other people slouched I just want to run up and fix them! But I don't of course! When I schedule time for writing and blogging I set a timer. I only work in one-and-a-half-hour increments. I get up and do something else. If I want to do more, I come back later in the day. It works for me.

GET OUTSIDE

Needless to say, I was not getting outside much during this time in my life. Taking a walk was out of the question. Even sitting in particular chairs was a problem. I tried to sit out on my patio as much as I could, but where I lived that is not a year-round activity. Everything had stopped. I wasn't able to attend my children's activities and events for a long while, and I was rarely doing anything social with friends or family. By the time I got to my Happiness Project, I had read enough to know managing stress is key to good mental and physical health. So my next monthly resolution would be to get outside. This would include being in nature and with actual people!

Did you know social interaction is a *huge* boost to your longevity? Being disconnected from community is worse for your health than smoking or obesity. It's a killer in its own right. No wonder I was feeling so awful. I was spending a ton of time alone. Doctor visits and seeing my family was the extent of my social time until I started my exercise classes. Those classes were the beginning, and I will write more about that later. My second month looked like this:

This Month's Resolution: Get Outside
My Quotation: "Be Active, Be Healthy, Be Happy."

Daily/Weekly Actions:
Plan a bird walk.
Be a local tourist.
Attend First Friday.
Find nature events.
Say yes.

Birding was an activity I discovered when moving to the East Coast from California. I was suddenly seeing birds I'd never seen before, which got me interested in bird-watching. Since we moved I've had multiple feeders and birdbaths. I would take guided bird walks in local parks to see different birds. I have to admit I'm still working on this one. I was hesitating for a long time for two reasons. The first reason was the walking. The second reason was I was concerned about looking up for two hours and the effect on my neck. This sounds like an ABCDE moment.

Being a local tourist is something I've *always* loved to do. And living near the nation's capital allows me access to many activities. This was an easy one. I'm a planner by nature. I'd just do what I had always done: look for local events and attractions and go! Attending my local area's First Friday event was something I always had penciled in on my calendar but didn't do. I was fearful of what all the walking would do to my back. But I needed to start getting out there, so I did it. My husband and I attended a

First Friday event where we visited local galleries, had a light dinner outside, listened to live music and just chatted as we roamed the streets. Yes, my back and neck flared up some, but it was worth it and I was exposing myself slowly to allowing my brain to realize this was going to be the new normal.

Being in nature was never a priority for me before. Ever. I wasn't a camper or a hiker or outdoorsy in any way. But now I realized the impact of nature and being outside on my mental and physical health, so on the list it went. When I say "Find Nature Events," that meant anything outside. I went to local fairs and festivals, plant sales, anything I could find that took place outdoors.

Did you ever say no to an invitation without any real reason to? I did this all the time. I am lucky enough to have many friends in this great community I live in, and I am positive that over the years I said no more than yes to invitations that came my way. Not to say I wasn't social, but I could have been doing so much more. This was a big one, and one that made an impact on my life. I started saying yes to every invitation. I also became that person who actually nails down a day and time when ideas for getting together are floated about. You know how it goes. You are chatting with friends and someone says, "We should do that sometime!" or "We should all go to … !" It all sounds great and then nothing happens. I became the person who would immediately send a text or an email to get the "thing" organized so it would happen. So, with the combination of saying yes to invitations and being the organizer, I suddenly had a social life again. And it was *great*. Saying yes is an affirmation I still use in meditation sometimes. It's easy for me to slip into "I don't feel like it." Even when I've made plans with someone and I don't feel like going, I remember my reasons (my why) and force myself to go. And guess what? I never regret it. It's always so energizing to be social. I'm learning a lot of these lessons later in life—well, mid-life—but I thank God I'm learning them at all. Life can be so much better.

Would you like to get outside more often? Try finding local events (a lot of which are free), go for a walk in nature at a local park and *say yes* to those invites you get!

IMPROVING MY HOME LIFE

This month was really about habit change. Our environments really do influence our productivity and mood. My favorite Gretchen Rubin quote ever is: "Outer order leads to inner calm." So true. Maybe people talk about the small act of making the bed having a big impact on their day. We feel it. I certainly do. When did I stop making my bed and why? It takes almost no time and is incredibly satisfying. I feel like the day is starting off well. One accomplishment done.

When I was stuck in my cycle of pain the last thing I felt like doing was chores around the house. Everything got done, trust me, and to an outsider it probably wasn't noticeable. But I noticed and I didn't like it. So this month's resolution would be improving my home life, which looked like this:

> This Month's Resolution: Improving My Home Life
>
> My Quotation: "Being organized isn't about getting rid of everything you own or trying to become a different person; it's about living the way you want, but better."
>
> **Daily/Weekly Actions:**
> Take care of dishes immediately.
> Take care of trash immediately.
> Make my bed every day.

These may seem like small things, but they had a big impact when I actually put them into motion. Clutter affects your mind and your stress levels. Read more about that here: https://www.mayoclinic.org/healthy-lifestyle/stress-management/in-depth/

how-decluttering-your-space-could-make-you-healthier-and-happier/
art-20390064.

Never having dishes in the sink makes the entire kitchen look clean and gives me a happiness boost. Maybe you don't use a lot of dishes every day, but I actually run my dishwasher three times a day. I cook a lot, and I have two teenagers who are constantly eating and one teen who enjoys cooking herself. The dishes get out of control quickly. My goal was to take care of them immediately. Same with the trash. In our house trash needs to be taken down a flight of stairs to go out, so it's a little inconvenient. I got a little lazy about it. "I'll take it later," I'd say to myself. And you might be asking why isn't anyone else in my household doing this chore? I'm the one there most of the time during the day. They are not. It doesn't make sense to wait around for someone else to do a chore when I can just get it done myself.

And I have already written about making the bed. I love a made bed! It just screams "I'm ready for the day!" Overall I just needed to get my house back in order after ignoring it for so long. Like I said, it was always clean, but just not organized the way it had been in the past and I missed that. The goal here was happiness, and the way things were looking around my house was not making me happy. These resolutions were not difficult, but important to my overall happiness. And I'm still working on this all the time. I have a home project notebook that has my lists of all my organizing ideas and repairs that need to be done around the house. There is always something to improve at home. The other day I decided to redecorate with items I already have. This is one of my favorite things to do when I get the shopping bug or the urge to do big redecorating. I will move some furniture around, hang pictures or move existing pictures to other parts of the house, rearrange knick-knacks, and bring things out of closets and cabinets to give them the light of day and find a place for them to bring life into our home. It always does the trick for me. When I'm done I stand back and smile. Are you thinking about decluttering your home? Try the following:

- If you don't already, make your bed every day and see how it makes you feel.

- Keep living areas decluttered by taking care of messes as they happen. Don't procrastinate! You will be surprised at how little time this takes. Another little tip is to listen to an audiobook or podcast when doing these types of chores.

BECOME AN OPTIMIST

After reading *Learned Optimism* and learning how to use the ABCDE method to start changing my pessimistic views and to overcome fears, I wanted to continue with this theme. I made it my next resolution:

> This Month's Resolution: Become an Optimist
> My Quotation: "You can't live a positive life with a negative mind."
>
> **Daily/Weekly Actions:**
> Problem solve.
> Pick a time of day to think.
> Listen to the *Happier* podcast.

The first action was to problem solve. Not my strong suit. It was rare that I actually would attack a problem in my life. I would skirt around it or make small changes, but I never would take the big, sweeping action steps necessary to solve a problem all the way. Problem-solving was part of my "How to Improve Coping Skills" list as well. Here's more on why problem-solving is important. "Work out what you need to do now to get over what has happened to you. Talk to people and think about taking practical steps, such as finding a support group. Sympathy feels good, and sometimes it's tempting to be a victim and tell people how bad your troubles are, but problem-solving will be more constructive in the long run." This sounds very much like something a child should have learned, something I should have learned along the way at some point but did not.

I wrote notes next to this action that say "budgeting—research in the fall." Money was at the forefront of my mind. We've always had plenty of money. My husband works very hard and is very successful—we thought the money never ended so we could spend and charge as we pleased. Not the case. That does catch up with you. I also had mounting medical bills of thousands of dollars with no end in sight. It was incredibly stressful. These notes represent the first time I thought about taking control of our financial situation. Our son would be leaving for college the next year, and we had put money away for him, but not nearly enough. And the thought of taking on additional debt made my stomach turn. Even though I did not take action on this immediately, I eventually did. I woke up to the fact that we could not continue on this path. I was adamant that no one was going to have debt, not my kids with student loans, and not us either.

For the first time in my life I started a budget. I did my research and found a few extremely helpful podcasts such as *HerMoney* with Jean Chatzky and *How to Money*. I took it all in, started my budget and attacked the debt. I started seriously saving, not just for college for my kids, but for everything coming our way in the next five years. I sold a ton of stuff and I cut expenses, but mostly I paid attention to where the money was going. I discovered we were wasting money *everywhere*. Throwing it away. Having a budget at first seems restrictive, but it's not. I've never felt so free to spend in my life. I felt not an ounce of guilt with any purchase because it was all accounted for. I'm happy to say we are just about debt free now and the college savings are building. Before I actually wrote down my resolution and took action, I would have never started this process. It would have been just another source of stress in my life, which was the last thing I needed at the time.

My second action, pick a time of day to think, was straight out of *Learned Optimism*. The idea was to use this time not to fret, but to problem solve and find solutions. This forced me to stop stressing out every time something came up. I would put it aside and have a time—for me, usually in the evening—when I would sit down and sort through all the issues that had come up. Even though I might not come up with a solution immediately, I hadn't spent my whole day in a state of worry. Read more about this strategy here: https://www.huffpost.com/entry/stop-worrying-anxiety-cycle_n_4002914.

My third action was to listen to the *Happier* podcast with Gretchen Rubin. When I started this Happiness Project, I began looking into the work Gretchen Rubin had done since I had read the original *Happiness Project* book eight years earlier. I found she had written several more books and now hosted a weekly podcast. I *devoured* these episodes. I had about two years' worth to listen to. To catch up, I listened whenever I could. Gretchen had many fun tips and hacks that I will go into more later. But for the most part having this podcast in my ear all the time kept some of my priorities in order and kept me on track. I can say the same about the personal finance podcasts. Podcasts are my new favorite thing! I rarely watch TV anymore. Podcasts are where it's at. No matter what niche you are into, there is a podcast for it, I promise. I've learned *so* much. I can't recommend them enough. Also, it's just so easy to have them on while getting ready in the morning, doing chores around the house or driving.

One more note about becoming an optimist. I just want to share another piece from *Learned Optimism*. Here Seligman provides the case against pessimism:

Pessimism promotes depression.

Pessimism produces inertia rather than activity in the face of setbacks.

Pessimism feels bad subjectively (blue, down, worried, anxious).

Pessimism is self-fulfilling. Pessimists don't persist in the face of challenges, and therefore fail more frequently—even when success is attainable.

Pessimism is associated with poor physical health.

"Even when pessimist are right and things turn out badly, they still feel worse. Their explanatory style now converts the predicted setback into a disaster, a disaster into a catastrophe." Who wants to live this way? Not me. I decided I never want to live like this again. My health was and is my number one priority and this was part of being healthy. Do you feel like you are a pessimist? Try the following:

- Use the ABCDE method covered earlier to change your mindset. It's life changing!

- Pick a time of day to think.

- Listen to a positive, motivating podcast to keep you on the right track. Having a daily reminder is so helpful!

BECOMING MINDFUL

Meditation and mindfulness were on my list of good mental health practices. At this point I began meditating a few minutes a day. My trainer had recommended an app that was very easy to use. She really was pushing meditation for me and I can see why. We have already established that I needed to *calm down*. And I now understood that this was going to be a part of my healing. It was time to get serious about mindfulness. My next resolution looked like this:

> This Month's Resolution: Become Mindful
> My Quotation: "Train your mind to see the good in every situation."
>
> **Daily/Weekly Actions:**
> Meditate daily.
> Take an online meditation course.
> Eat mindfully/live in the moment.

I didn't know when I started meditating the awesome power it has. It has made an enormous impact on my life. I started with just a few minutes a day and worked my way up from there. I also began a sleep meditation at night, which was fantastic! No more busy brain keeping me up at night. I turn on the guided meditation and I'm asleep in minutes! Heavenly. After I found a few guided meditations on the app I was using I discovered Deepak Chopra's 21 Day Meditation Experience. Have you ever done one of these programs? Let me explain. Every few months Deepak provides these 21 Day Meditation programs for free. I still can't believe they are free for the amount of content and the quality you get. Each program presents a topic to work on within the twenty-one days. First, and most of the time, each day begins with an introduction from Oprah speaking to us with all her wisdom. I'm a big Oprah fan! Then we hear from Deepak. Both he and Oprah explain the topic at hand. I take *a lot* of notes during this time!

Next, Deepak gives us listeners a centering thought, something to carry us through the day and to remember from the day's teachings. Then we prepare to meditate. We sit, breath and listen. Deepak gives us a mantra to silently repeat to ourselves during the meditation, which will last approximately fifteen minutes. When the meditation is completed, there are journaling questions to ask yourself and reflect on. This practice really spoke to me. I could feel after the twenty-one days a calmness that wasn't there before. It was noticeable when I realized that instead of getting worked up, angry or anxious about things, I would be more in the flow. I didn't get so excited about the little things that can and do go wrong in life. That was my meditation practice showing up for me.

Meditation has so many benefits. To name a few, it reduces pain, boosts your immune system, generates feelings of optimism, releases fear and anxiety, helps control thoughts and emotions, improves focus and helps you relax and sleep better. I needed every single one of those things and more. If you want to read more about the science behind the benefits of meditation, you can find out more here: https://www.washingtonpost.com/news/inspired-life/wp/2015/05/26/harvard-neuroscientist-meditation-not-only-reduces-stress-it-literally-changes-your-brain/ I have learned and grown so much over the past two years, and most of that is due to my meditation practice, which leads to self-awareness and personal growth. The overall effect has been that I no longer get so anxious or panicky. A simple thing could set me off in the past. Thankfully, I haven't had any episodes since I started my practice. Have you ever had a panic attack? It basically feels like you're dying. It's the most awful out-of-body experience and I hope to never feel like that again. I don't think I will because I have so many tools to work with now.

This leads to my next action, which was to take on online meditation course. There are so many online classes! Some are free and some aren't. I chose a free, well-reviewed course and was not disappointed. I recommend this for anyone new to meditation. I loved the way the instructor taught all the different types of meditation, because they do vary. I scheduled time in my calendar every day to do the lessons. It didn't take much time and I truly enjoyed it. If you would like to check it out, click here: https://palousemindfulness.com/.

Eat mindfully/live in the moment falls into just being present. I started to pay attention to the current moment rather than reliving events of the past or worrying about the future. You really can beat anxiety by just being present. Eating mindfully, or doing whatever it is you are doing at the moment, keeps you present. Also, this forced me to stop multitasking—there is no such thing. One activity always suffers and you end up doing two or more things badly instead of one well. Eating doesn't require any skill, but the idea of eating mindfully is to enjoy food without rushing or standing at the kitchen counter. I was not only practicing eating mindfully, but single-tasking in general. You can read about that here: https://www.psychologytoday.com/us/blog/the-power-prime/201103/technology-myth-multitasking. Have you thought about meditating? If you would like to become more mindful, try the following:

- Take an online or in-person meditation course.

- Make meditation a part of your daily schedule.

- Practice single-tasking.

DO FOR OTHERS

Did you know volunteering has many health benefits? Not only are you helping someone or a cause in need you are also receiving as much as you are giving. Studies show volunteering improves the immune system, lowers blood pressure, reduces chronic pain, lowers levels of depression, decreases risk of heart disease and increases longevity by up to ten years! That's quite a list!

Again, why would I not do this? This was another mental health/coping skill I was determined to work on. For years I did some volunteering. I was very active in my children's schools with the PTA and in the classroom, and I would donate clothes and food to various organizations. But I never volunteered for something I was truly passionate about. Obviously I cared about my children's school, but I needed to do more. This month's resolution was:

This Month's Resolution: Do for Others
My Quotation: "Helping one person might not change the whole world, but it could change the world for one person."

Daily/Weekly Tasks:
Volunteer.

Simply volunteer, but in a big way. Later in my journey I worked through how I came upon a lot of the groups I'm involved in now and how volunteering became a huge part of my life. But at the time of my Happiness Project I immediately thought of working with senior citizens in some way. I had met quite a few seniors in my time at the exercise classes I was attending. They were the most caring, honest people I had ever met. I loved them! So I researched opportunities in my county and found a meal delivery service for seniors who cannot get out to a senior center for lunch. I signed up to deliver meals once a month to start. This turned out to be just what I needed. Volunteering is another stress reliever. I was still in quite a bit of pain at this time and driving was uncomfortable. But I put that aside when I was delivering. I loved meeting all the seniors and having a little chat with them about their day. And I was being *useful*. They were helping me and didn't know it. Volunteering has come to mean so much more to me now. I have a greater awareness of myself and my purpose. At the time, this was just the beginning. I was thrilled to be doing anything other than focusing on my body and my pain.

Volunteering can be contagious. Shortly after I started, my dad began delivering meals as well, and then my mom joined the Red Cross and started working blood drives—all positive effects on me, the people I was helping and my immediate family. Looking outside myself and my own problems is huge. When you are volunteering, you are distracted and you're thinking of others. Another benefit for me was the social interaction. I had interaction now, more than the year before, but I knew I needed more. This filled that need as well. Social connection is another indicator of longevity. We are learning now that low social connection can be as detrimental on our health as smoking or being obese! Volunteering gets you out into the world for the benefit of all. Have you thought about volunteering more? Try the following:

- Research your local government website for opportunities.
- Think about what you are interested in and research from there.
- Are there opportunities at your church? Or your school?

ART LOVER

I have always been a patron of the arts. As far back as I can remember, I was and remain an enormous music fan. I bought my first 45 at eight years old (yes, I'm showing my age here) and my love of music and live performances grew from there. When I was a child, my parents regularly took me to museums, foreign and independent films, art exhibits and festivals. These adventures stuck with me through adulthood. I spend a lot of time seeking these things out for myself and my family. It wasn't and isn't unusual for me to plan an entire trip to another city just to see an exhibit. We have done this as a family countless times. I don't know if my kids will inherit this love of the arts. I can only hope!

During the time when I was not functional, all the fun stuff was off the table. I could not even entertain the thought of traipsing through a museum or going to a concert. So, while working on my Happiness Project, I thought I needed to get back to doing what I love as soon as possible.

This Month's Resolution: The Arts
My Quotation: "The purpose of art is washing the dust of daily life off our souls."

Daily/Weekly Actions:
Attend live performances.
Find a craft I can learn.
Listen to music every day.
Seek out exhibits.

First up, attend live performances! Well, I certainly have done that! I started with a few concerts and other live events and, to be honest, sitting in those chairs for hours was brutal on my neck at first. And it was frustrating and depressing. But I enjoyed getting out to do what I loved so much that I kept going. I kept getting physical therapy to get myself through. Eventually that didn't happen anymore. It took awhile. Probably eight months. Now I don't even think about it; I just go and have a good time. Did you know people who attend concerts live longer! Just saying …

Finding a craft was a tough one. I love being crafty, but I'm not exactly good at it. The ladies from my exercise group invited me to an art class and I thought *Yay! This is exactly what I've been looking to do!* I'm not going to say I created a masterpiece. It was pretty rough. But the experience made me feel happy and connected to these ladies. That was the first of many outings we did together! We have a standing lunch date once a month now that I treasure. We also have an annual summertime tradition of seeing a show at a local venue. I'm always looking forward to our time together! And for the record, I'm still searching for a craft. I tried drawing and sketching, but got bored with it. I enjoy bullet journaling, and that can be crafty. I'm still on the hunt.

Listening to music every day came in the form of Spotify. I was an iTunes user until my son explained how much music I could access with Spotify. He could not understand why I was not using it! Once I got used to it I was sold! Now I'm not sure how I did without it! Listening to music is the ultimate distraction. I listen in the car, while I'm cooking or in the middle of doing laundry. I listen anytime I can, just because it makes me so happy.

I'm lucky to live near the nation's capital. I could not ask for a better place to seek out exhibits. There is *constantly* something wonderful to see! Really, it's just a matter of having the time to get there to see it. I head to the city at least once a month to see an exhibit or a show. DC is full of museums, most of which are free. I get excited to see the Arts Preview section of the newspaper every season, sitting down with my cup of tea and circling all the things I want to attend over the next few months! It's the best!

How about you? What do you love doing? Maybe it's not the arts. Maybe it's sporting events, or dog shows, or car shows. Think about what you love to do and make a plan to do more of it. I promise it will make you happier!

SPIRITUALITY

At this point one thing was clear. I needed a jump start on my spirituality practice. Over the years my practice changed. As a child, I had no practice whatsoever, coming from a home of agnostics. Even that has changed as my parents' personal journey has evolved. But I'm not here to tell their story, only mine. My husband was raised Catholic. We did not discuss religion much at all when we were dating. I was pretty clear about my agnostic ways, but we had no real discussion until we were expecting our first child. Suddenly it was very important to my husband that we raise our children Catholic and that I also convert. I agreed to take the classes. I actually found myself drawn to it. Looking back, I probably would have been drawn to any spiritual practice at that point just because I was starved for it but didn't realize what I was missing. For many years we went to our local Catholic church and enrolled the kids in Confraternity of Christian Doctrine (CCD) classes. I joined a playgroup with the moms of the church. A lot of good came out of those years. I certainly needed the moms. As a new mom not knowing many women in my neighborhood (as I was working until my pregnancy) I needed their help and support. I was the only new mom of the group. I got recommendations on preschools, advice on parenting and the friendship of seeing these women every week for about two years. Over time, though, my husband and I grew dissatisfied with the organization as a whole and could no longer stay. We then attended a local Methodist church for a few years that all of us really liked. I found it very welcoming and even joined a ladies' Bible study. I began a daily spiritual practice of praying, reflecting upon my day and reading the Bible. The leadership of that church changed and our kids grew older. Slowly we stopped going altogether.

I continued my daily practice for a few years after we stopped attending church services. As I was suffering through all the pain of my situation, I continued this practice, but I was craving so much more. With this in mind, I devoted a month to spirituality.

This Month's Resolution: Spirituality
My Quotation: "Spiritual growth involves giving up the stories of your past so the universe can write a new one."

Daily/Weekly Actions
Pray every day.
Practice gratitude.

That was it. If I was to write this list now, I would include meditation under spirituality because I don't feel they should be separated. At the time, though, this seemed right. It was just the beginning.

Prayer comes in a different form for me today. Every morning I start my day with a ten- to twenty-minute meditation. Sometimes it's another gratitude practice, thanking the universe for what I have. Prayer can be walking in nature or the quiet moments in yoga when everything is coming together and I'm being extremely mindful. These are all spiritual practices to me. I will go much deeper into this later when I write about how I began to grow in my spiritual practice.

I'm sure you have heard about the miraculous changes that occur with regular gratitude practice. I desperately needed this. When I sit down every night to write five things I'm grateful for that day, it is nearly impossible to stay upset or wallow in my own misery. There are *always* things to be grateful for, even when things aren't going well. There is always something. Some days are harder than others, but those things are still there. Even if it's just the beautiful birds at my feeder. I don't find myself wanting more stuff anymore. That desire is gone. I have plenty. When you start to be grateful for what you have everything shifts.

Do you have a spiritual practice? If you would like to begin, I suggest the following. This is not a one-size-fits-all situation. It's very personal, so do what you feel is best for you. Some things to explore include:

- Your local church.
- Daily prayer.
- Daily gratitude practice.
- Meditation.
- Time to Read

Reading had been put on the back burner because of my neck issues. Anytime I sat down to read for more than a few minutes, my neck would flare up. This was extremely depressing. It was one more thing taken from me during this time. And something that gave me so much joy. I knew I had to start slowly, like with everything else. My resolution looked like this:

This Month's Resolution: Reading
My Quotation: "You can't buy happiness, but you can buy books, and that's kind of the same thing."

Daily/Weekly Actions:
Read in the morning.
Take my book everywhere.
Set goals.
Schedule reading into my calendar.

Let me start by saying I've *always* loved to read, since childhood. I went through phases when I read less (e.g., my teens and new motherhood), but the love was always there. There's nothing like getting deeply lost in a book. It really made me dislike movies for awhile. With a book I can get so deep into a character's thoughts that movies just seemed superficial. But I can respect movies now as an art form. I'm just very selective about what I see and I tend to lean toward documentaries.

Reading in the morning when it's quiet and no one else is up is one of the best parts of my day. I have my tea, I run through my phone to make sure nothing major is going on, I meditate, and then I read. Sometimes that morning reading time is the only chance I get all day to read; at other times I can pick up my book again and again. As long as I read in the morning, I know I will get some reading time in no matter what the day has in store for me.

Having a book with me at all times results in a much better use of my time than scrolling around mindlessly on my phone. For example, I will read when I am waiting at an appointment, sitting at the car wash or just about anywhere. I just throw my book into my bag before I leave for wherever I'm going that day.

I set reading goals in two ways. I use the Goodreads app to track all of the books I've read, and I also use it to set my yearly reading goals. My yearly goal for many years was twenty. A lot of times I didn't hit that. But once I had more specific goals and, most importantly, stopped watching TV almost altogether, that's when the real progress came. My yearly goal last year was fifty and I went a little over, so this year I set it for sixty. Currently I'm on track for completing it. Back to TV. I learned a little something from Laura VanderKam about time management. If you haven't read her book *168 Hours*, I highly recommend it. TV is a *big* time killer. All the things we think we don't have time to do can probably be done with the elimination or the scheduling of TV watching. The first thing I did was stop using TV for background noise. If I'm doing chores at home, I will play an audiobook or a podcast, both of which I enjoy much more than TV. There are TV shows I like! But now I record them, then I schedule time on my calendar once or twice a week to watch them. That's it. No more hours and hours of whatever is on. My TV watching is purposeful. This is a real game changer for time management. It's allowed me to complete my online health coaching certification without any disruption to my life. It's also allowed me to write this book! I've taken on many, many activities since my second Happiness Project, and I'm asked all the time how I have the energy and time to do everything. I was able to accomplish this for a few reasons. One, of course, is scheduling TV watching. Two, I'm an Upholder as I've said before. When I decide to do something, I jump in and do it. Three, I'm a planner. I love filling up my calendar with all my goals and to-dos!

The second reading goal I set was new to me in the past year or so. When I mentioned it to my daughter she said, "That's how we do it in school!" I honestly don't know where I picked up this tip, but it's been very helpful in moving my reading along. I don't set an amount of *time* to read—I set a page number goal. For example, I used to jot down that I would read for thirty minutes or an hour in my reading calendar. Sometimes I would complete that time and sometimes I wouldn't. But when I changed the goal to "read fifty (or one hundred) pages" I always completed it. It didn't matter how long it took. When I made this change I started flying through books. Usually I have a fiction and a nonfiction book going at the same time. I usually am listening to an audiobook as well. Three books at once. This is how I hit my reading goals. I have an extremely long "to be read" list! And did I mention I work part-time in a library surrounded by books calling my name and discovering books I may never have sought out on my own? This is a huge happiness boost!

My neck is becoming accustomed to reading again. I will admit that I no longer have marathon reading days. To be honest, I miss that. But I know I would pay the price with neck pain if I read for an entire day. It's all about making it work. What I have set up for myself is working and has increased my happiness, and that was the goal to start with! Do you want to read more? Try the following:

- Visit your local library. Libraries are wonderful! So many books for you to choose from. Visit your local libraries' websites to search for e-books and audiobooks. There truly is no reason to buy a book, with one exception. I still buy books if I plan to have that book signed by the author (which I do often). Everything else comes from the library.

- Try reading in the morning before your day gets going. If time is tight in the morning, consider waking up thirty minutes earlier to fit it in.

- Set your own personal goals. I'll go back to Gretchen Rubin here and suggest you know your personality type. That will help you build your habits in a way that will work for your personality.

VISION BOARDS

Remember when everyone was doing vision boards after Oprah talked about them back in the day? I remember wanting to do one, but never did, until 2017. I was in the middle of my Happiness Project and decided a vision board would be a great way for me to have a constant reminder of all the things I wanted to focus on not only for the new year but also in my future life. I'm going to break down my vision board into sections so I can go a little deeper into each goal/vision. Some goals will need their own section like this one, but others won't.

Here's what I came up with! This was a lot of fun to make. I researched all the things I wanted to focus on and found pictures and quotes to cut out and paste to my board. I also bought some motivational stickers for fun.

I started with new friends. I have already written about finding my tribe; now I was on a mission to curate that in my life. I look at the people I meet differently now too. Let's look at the whole list.

NEW FRIENDS

1. REALIZE YOUR FEAR IS IN YOUR HEAD. (It's not as scary as you think.)

    This is most certainly true. It's not scary at all, actually. I'm not a shy person. It's not that I was afraid to make new friends. I just didn't want to. I didn't see the value, so I didn't bother getting to know new people. I know how awful this sounds. But I'm being honest. I didn't realize the *richness* of having the *right* friends in your life makes all the difference.

2. START WITH PEOPLE YOU KNOW. (Reach out to acquaintances, join existing groups, meet friends' friends, accept social invitations.)

    I did start reaching out to those friends I already had who I missed and wanted to keep in my life. I started inviting those people to lunch, shows, movies, etc., just to see them. And in return I said yes when invited to any social function. One thing I really focused on was saying yes. I made sure that if I was invited to something, I said yes. Unless there was a good reason, like a scheduling conflict, I went. This changed everything. Just going and doing opens up your world and makes your life so rich. It's actually shocking when I think back to the times I said no for no reason whatsoever. I just didn't want to. Or I wanted to and decided it wasn't worth the effort. I'll admit sometimes I'll have a commitment and think *I really don't feel like doing this*. But I'm *always* glad I did. I'm usually energized and sometimes I meet new people I adore, which is the whole point, isn't it?

3. GET YOURSELF OUT THERE. (Join meet-up groups, attend courses, volunteer, go to parties.)

    I took this one to heart. I dove into my volunteer groups. Some stuck and some didn't. That's okay because the ones that stuck have brought so much to my life. And I'm always on the lookout for meet-up groups.

4. TAKE THE FIRST STEP. (Say hello—it's about being sociable.)
    This was not a reach for me. I was already doing this.

5. BE OPEN. (Don't judge; on an emotional level, open your heart.)
    I feel like I was already pretty open. The difference now is that I was authentic.

6. GET TO KNOW THE PERSON. (What does he/she do? What are his/her values? What are his/her passions? Goals? Dreams? What motivates/drives him/her?)

    Because I'm so aware of this goal of mine to build my tribe, when I meet someone new I hear myself asking a ton of questions. I *never* used to do that. I would be polite, and if I did find myself having a good time with someone, I typically just told stories about myself as much as possible. My ego was definitely in charge! Now I ask a lot of questions to get to know people quickly and well. This is a realization I had recently. Once I start getting to know someone by asking questions and being interested in their life, I find I'm suddenly making plans with people I had just met that day! What a happiness boost that is! Or if I'm talking to someone I know fairly well and we both realize we have something in common, I now immediately suggest an outing together. I can't tell you the number of times I've done this and it's resulted in the most fun days and experiences—not only with new friends but with old ones too.

7. CONNECT WITH PEOPLE GENUINELY. (Warmth, love and respect build friendship.) I check in on my friends more often now. If I'm thinking of them, I send a quick text to see how they are doing, try to make plans and just generally let them know I'm thinking of them.

8. BE YOURSELF. (Don't change yourself for anyone else.) This was a big lesson for me. I was pretty good at morphing into whatever I needed to be (or thought I needed to be) in a social situation. Most of the time I kept my views to myself so I didn't offend anyone. I did this for years. Someone would be going off about something I completely disagreed with and I would not say anything because I thought that's the polite thing to do. I'm not saying I'm rude now, but I do speak my mind. I don't hide from how I feel. I put it all out there and then people can decide for themselves if they are willing to have an honest and intelligent conversation. No one is better at explaining the importance of this than Brene Brown. I'm a big fan of her work and highly suggest checking her out if you aren't familiar with her.

9. BE THERE FOR THEM. (That's what friendship is about.) I try to be there for my friends when they need help. I offer more often than I used to. I make a point of checking in if I know they are struggling with something. Offer rides, time to chat or words of support. It makes a difference.

10. MAKE THE EFFORT TO STAY IN TOUCH. (It takes two to clap.) I actually schedule "keeping in touch" on my calendar. I have a running list of people I want to connect with, and this is

a little reminder to get in touch with them before too much time goes by.

All of these steps have enriched my life. I've made some really good friends. I'm more social than ever, and it truly is a happiness boost. Remember back on my "Good Mental Health" list was "Friendship." These smaller steps are helping me reach my overall larger goal of health and wellness to in part, retrain my brain and to build coping skills to attain that goal.

Have you made a vision board? Consider making one to focus on your personal aspirations. Vision boards certainly aren't the only way to achieve goals, but I find they are a really good tool to remind you of why you are doing what you are doing. That's what my vision board did for me. Try the following:

- Gather up all your supplies to make your board: poster board, stickers, magazine clippings, articles/info you find on the Internet or anything else you find inspiring.

- Create your board!

- Place your board where you will see it every single day. It will be a constant reminder of your intentions and will prompt you to act.

PART 4

AWAKENING

My First 21 Day Meditation Experience

TIME

I'm not sure how I came upon my first 21 Day Meditation Experience with Deepak Chopra, but I do know it came at the right time. Because I was so new to meditation and had just begun using my new Insight Timer app, I was open to learning more. So when I saw this I immediately signed up. If you aren't familiar with the programs Deepak Chopra offers, they are in collaboration with Oprah and guide you through twenty-one days of mantras, meditation, self-discovery and journaling. I find them incredibly useful. I have learned so much about myself from these programs. And did I mention they are free? It's amazing the number of aha moments that came out of these experiences for me. I have everything written in my notebook, and I can see where the learning happened and how I moved forward with it and the changes I made in my current life because of it. Pretty powerful stuff! Here are my thoughts and lessons learned throughout my first 21 Day Meditation Experience.

Each session has a theme. The first one I did was time. I had a lot of lessons to learn here. The first lesson was "making every moment matter." On Day 1 Deepak said, "If you don't have enough time, you need to manage it better." Yes, of course!

DAY 1 THREE THINGS I WANT TO HAVE MORE TIME FOR:

- My husband.
- Volunteering.
- Having fun.

Three things that feel like lost or wasted time:

- Household chores.
- Scrolling on my phone.
- TV.

The goal here was to achieve a more fulfilling use of time while decreasing wasted time. I decided to make use of my early afternoons and evenings volunteering or doing something fun. I took this to heart and these things are now all happening in my life. Doing something fun also allowed me to spend time with my husband. Two for one! We make a regular habit of going to concerts, as we are both music lovers. He played in a band in a previous life and I was a music lover surrounded by musicians in my youth (my husband being one of them!). We have a deep love for music. This is our thing.

Volunteering was the other area I wanted to make more time for in my life. I did a little research and found a meal delivery service for homebound seniors. This was a county program where I could make my own schedule. It was a perfect start to volunteering. I love seniors! They are the most honest, funny, lovable people! It made my day to deliver their meals and chat a little. Doing for others is so important for both the people you are helping and your overall health. Win-win.

As far as lost or wasted time was concerned, I decided household chores are inevitable, so I would make the most of them by listening to a podcast or audiobook while I am cleaning. No more TV on in the background. I go days without watching TV now. I don't miss it at all. I record my shows, and when I schedule the time to watch, I get my fill. You can do anything you want to do if you take control of your TV habits.

Phone scrolling is the same. I started setting a timer when I would sit down and scroll through my phone in the morning and evening. If I don't, an hour can go by just like that! I could have been reading, writing, exercising, meditating or any of the other things I want to bring into my life. I'm still working on this habit. I still forget to set my timer sometimes. I need to set a reminder for my timer!

While on the subject of wasted time, I want to mention Laura Vanderkam and her books on time management. I found her work fascinating. She suggests keeping a time log for a few days to see how you are using your time. If you want to know where you are wasting time, just try it! My time log was eye-opening! Most clear was my unplanned time scrolling on my phone. It was all there in black and white. I want to accomplish a lot, and the only way to do that is to manage my time well. This is an area that I have to continually come back to for review and get back on track. Here's a link to Laura Vanderkam's TED Talk if you want to know more: https://www.ted.com/talks/laura_vanderkam_how_to_gain_control_of_your_free_time?utm_source=tedcomshare&utm_medium=email&utm_campaign=tedspread. Do you feel like you have lost or wasted time in your day? Try the following:

- Keep a log of your time using Laura Vanderkam's method or choose one of your own.

- List the things you want to make more time for. Keep the list small, just three or four things.

- List areas of wasted or lost time.

- Think of ways to use your time more wisely so as to increase what you want to bring into your life and to decrease lost or wasted time.

DAY 2 FLOW

Day 2 of my meditation experience was all about staying in the present moment and being in the flow of life. Deepak said, "The present moment is filled with new possibilities." He was saying that we can do more in the moment to be happy. I'm always working on paying attention and being in the moment. Deepak was asking me to think of three things I get totally absorbed in that I love. When I lose track of time, that's being in the flow. It's good to recognize those things that create a state of flow for you. Mine were:

- Meditation.

- Exercise.

- Reading.

I've already written a lot about meditation. It is most definitely a place where I can lose track of time. Not always, but a lot of the time I "go somewhere else." It's the best feeling of calm and transcendence.

When I'm exercising I am *very* present, especially when exercising in a group class. If I was at home, I could let my mind wander and it didn't really matter (or least I didn't think it did) if I lost track of what I was doing for a few minutes because I was daydreaming. Being in a group setting immediately makes you more present. I find I'm really in the flow in yoga class. Yoga is a meditation of its own. Being present is part of the practice.

The third area is reading. Do you ever get totally lost in a book? I do! If it's a good book, I get transported elsewhere and lose all track of time. This is when I began my focus on reading more clearly. As you have read previously, I utilize a couple of strategies for getting more reading into my day. I pledged to read in the early morning before starting my day and to take my book with me wherever I go. I have continued this along with other ways to increase my reading time over the past few years, and it's worked beautifully. Try the following:

- Take some time to think about activities in your life where you lose track of time.

- Plan to make more time for those activities by tracking your time.

DAY 3 LIVING IN THE NOW

Did you know if you are living in the present moment there can be no anxiety? How about that? If you are dwelling on the past or projecting into the future and it's making you stressed, focus on the present moment. Once I had this awareness, it helped my stress levels tremendously.

For years I spent so much time worrying. Mostly I worried about my kids, but somehow over the years, my anxiety levels grew into fears that weren't there before like fear of flying or going to the doctor. I was hyperaware of everything I needed to do as a mom to keep my kids safe, and that bled over into everything I did for myself. I suddenly felt afraid of so many things I wasn't before. I spent *a lot* of time worrying about the what-ifs with my kids. What if my son doesn't get selected for the team he wants to play on? What if my daughter's audition doesn't go well? What if a stranger approaches them? What if they get hurt? What if they get sick? What if, what if, what if … It's enough to drive a mother mad. We all do it. We love our kids and are going to protect them. Period. But living in fight-or-flight mode all the time will destroy your health. I simply could not continue that way. By the time I got to my own health problems I was at a very high stress level. And hearing "I don't know what's wrong with you" from doctors made me project into the future. I can see that now.

Dwelling on the past is just as destructive. Reliving old hurts does not help anyone. Do you know your brain doesn't know whether you are actually experiencing these moments or are just replaying them in your mind? The result is stress either way. Deepak says, "I restore inner balance when I live in the now." Yes, so true. And to do this is as easy as a one-minute breathing meditation. Guided meditations are available to use when you are experiencing a stressful moment and you need to bring yourself back to the present. I list some helpful apps later.

I can see now, looking back, that this mindset was affecting my health in many ways, slowly over time. I'm happy to be out of that place. I'm not saying I don't have fears now, but if I do, I have ways to work through them without getting upset or working myself up into a frenzy. Do you find yourself living in the past or the future? Is it causing unneeded stress and worry? Try the following:

- Download a meditation app. I like Insight Timer, but there are many (Calm, Headspace, 10% Happier). Use a guided meditation to bring you back to the present moment. Choosing just a one-minute breathing awareness meditation can be so helpful. You can always choose a longer one if you like.

- Make this a practice in your life and you will find yourself in a much calmer state of mind.

DAY 4 THE HEALING POWER OF SLEEP

Sleep is *so* important! You've heard this your entire life, right? But it truly is. We reset our natural biorhythms when we sleep and that is when we heal. Did you know meditation is the most important healing time, second only to sleep? This revelation inspired me to make sleep a priority for real. I made the following changes:

- I changed my cat's feeding schedule so she didn't wake me up so early. (This may seem like a small thing, but I wasn't going back to sleep after she woke me up, so it was huge!)

- I informed my family that they are *not* to wake me up after I've gone to sleep to tell me about the random things they need or want the next day. The kids seemed to remember all the important things they needed to tell me at 10–11 p.m. Now I have a system where if they need to tell me about something that needs to be taken care of first thing in the morning (waking them up early, needing a particular item of clothing clean, a permission slip that needs to be signed), they are to send me a text explaining it. Now I see their texts first thing in the morning, and they didn't need to wake me up. It works out great!

If you are at all doubting the importance of sleep, I highly suggest you listen to Ariana Huffington speak about her experience with sleep deprivation and what happened to her and the changes she's made in her life to make sleep a priority. It's her mission now to make people aware of the science behind getting enough sleep. Some people wear their sleep deprivation like a badge of honor, but I think that will start to change in our culture. You can still be a highly functioning, successful person *and* take care of your body. Totally doable. Do you feel like you are getting enough sleep? Are you making it a priority? Try the following:

- List the reasons why you may not be getting restful sleep.

- Think about how you could make the changes needed to help you get the sleep you need.

DAY 5 MEDITATION

Deepak said, "All renewal occurs in the now." At this point I had learned how important it is to stay present, and that meditation is a form of healing, just as sleep is. The focus for me now was to make it a priority in my life.

The science behind meditation is clear. The repetitive nature of meditating actually changes the pathways in your brain, which in turn creates a healthier you! To read more click here: https://www.webmd.com/balance/features/transcendental-meditation#1.

My takeaway here was a reinforcement of what I already knew. Meditation has to be a priority. It's nonnegotiable. I have seen changes in my behavior since I started my practice. Things that would send me off, stress me out or make me angry just don't anymore. I even surprise myself! I certainly had a moment at my daughter's dance competition a year or so ago that would have had the old me ranting and raving, angry and yelling. But I didn't. I remember thinking *It will all be fine.* I knew it would work out. But would it? The truth was I just wasn't worried or stressed about the outcome. I was in the flow and completely calm. This startled my mom, who was with me at the time. She said she couldn't believe how calm I was. If anyone has seen the old me, it's my mom! The calmness and the retraining of my brain that happens in my meditation had carried over into my everyday life. It's a wonderful thing! Do you have a meditation practice? Are you seeing results in your everyday life? Again, I suggest picking up a meditation practice if you haven't already done so!

- Download a meditation app such as Insight Timer, Headspace or Calm.

- Create a habit of meditating daily for one minute to start and build from there.

DAY 6 PRESENT MOMENT AWARENESS

Continuing my 21 Day Meditation Experience, Day 6 focused on going deeper into present moment awareness. Deepak said, "You must be present to give and receive love. If you are angry or gossiping, you are not in awareness." He suggested taking a few deep breaths to get back to the present anytime you are not in awareness. In my journaling that day I wrote down three things that take me out of present moment awareness:

- Multitasking.

- Worry.

- Interruptions.

I noted earlier that there is no such thing as multitasking. *Single* tasking as often as possible is my goal. I pay attention to what I'm doing, or more importantly, pay attention to whomever I'm speaking to—most often my children. Instead of reading, writing or creating my to-do list while my children are talking, my focus now is to stop what I'm doing and listen to them with my full attention. Not halfway. Single tasking. Multitasking made me feel accomplished. Look at me getting it all done so efficiently! But the truth is, multitasking results in two (or more) things being done poorly instead of one thing being done well. It's tempting to multitask. This is one issue I'm always working on. If I keep coming back to the "why," then it's easier to do.

Worry was absolutely taking me out of the present moment. There is no anxiety in the present moment. If I worry about something that could happen in the future or a past hurt, that will create unnecessary stress. If I caught myself doing that, I would refocus my attention to the now.

Interruptions are inevitable, but I try to minimize them as much as possible. If I have something I want to do uninterrupted, I plan to do it either when no one else is home or when I am alone elsewhere. This decreases the times the kids need their mom or my husband has a question about something or just wants to chat. I especially like uninterrupted reading time. And my favorite place to read is outdoors. I find it so relaxing. If I want to spend a significant amount of time writing, I also try to do this when no one else is home. Having an interruption when in the flow of writing is frustrating and can take me out of my thoughts, and it can take a while to get back to where I was before the interruption. How do you stay present? Try the following:

- Ask yourself what takes you out of present moment awareness.

- Ask yourself how you can make changes in your life to minimize interruptions.

DAY 7 IT'S NOT ME TALKING

Today's lesson in my 21 Day Meditation Experience was still concentrated on the present moment, but now also addressed observing your own thoughts. Years ago Oprah did an online course with Eckhart Tolle on his book *A New Earth*. This was my first foray into learning about the ego. Once you learn it, you can't unlearn it. I see it *everywhere* in myself, in others and in people I don't even know. I hear the ego speaking. If you recognize this voice as your false self, you can see that you are the observer of your thoughts. Deepak says, "We are not our thoughts." That is so true. Having this awareness was so enlightening! It drives home the idea that my true self is in my awareness, not my thoughts. If my thoughts are taking me down the road of worry and past hurts, that takes up my present time. I needed to learn how to be in the present as much as possible to keep stress and worry at bay. Deepak says three things take up the present moment.

- Dwelling on old regrets.
- Anticipating the future.
- Worry as protection.

I did all of these on a regular basis. Dwelling on old regrets was something I did occasionally, but not as much as the other two. Anticipating the future? All the time! All my "what if something happens to my kids" worries lay here. And until I heard this I never thought about worry as protection, but that's exactly what it is. It's preparation for disaster. I would say to myself, "If I think about it enough, it won't happen." It's exhausting really. I do not want to live that way ever again. And I'm happy to say I don't. At the moment, I have a parent who is dealing with some serious health issues. I'm surprising myself at how well I'm handling it. I'm not up all night with worry, I'm not projecting the future, I'm not thinking about it nonstop. It's truly incredible. The old me would be stressed to the point of not eating (a hallmark indicator of my stress levels back then), talking about the what-ifs constantly and obsessing over any information I could find on WebMD. I'm tired even reading this. No wonder I felt the way I did! Meditation carries over into real life and I'm living proof of that! Staying present is a big part of my practice. Do you find yourself not in the present moment? Think about trying the following: Remember only the "now" is real. If you find your self-talk is focused on old regrets or worry about the future, recognize this as your ego (your false self). You are not your thoughts.

DAY 8 PAST HURTS

Day 8 went a little deeper into old regrets. I wrote I didn't tend to do this as much as the other two, and that is true, but when I did let my brain wander this way, it was not good. Deepak said, "Old wounds get a new life when we think of hard times in the past." I experienced this when thinking of painful, traumatic events from my childhood. I had some not-so-great years when I was growing up. Sometimes these memories creep up at the most unexpected times. When they did I was reliving them, and I would grow nauseous and get an uncomfortable feeling in my body that is hard to describe. This happened when memories would come up about certain occasions in my teenage years—some very death-defying scary times—and suddenly my body is reacting. It's an odd feeling if you've never experienced it. According to Deepak, being in the present moment can heal the trauma from these experiences.

Broken relationships was another area of reliving old hurts that would come back and haunt me occasionally. Something would trigger a memory, and suddenly I was back in that place. Sometimes these incidents feel like they just happened, even though they happened thirty or more years ago! And of course the old hurt that was the most recent and most devastating was the injury itself. I wrote in my notebook: Drug reaction/physical pain/missed years.

It makes me sad to even read it. A lot of sadness and anger was there, so much time lost with my kids, family and friends. And time lost from doing all the things I love. I could not and would not dwell on this old hurt. I know now I can write about it and tell my story without being there.

These experiences all had lessons to teach me. In the case of my injuries, I had to learn it twice. As I wrote in the very beginning of this book, I had *two* episodes that took me out of commission for extended times. It was like I didn't learn my lesson well enough the first time around, so the universe said, "Let's try this again!" I get it now, I promise. After the first time, I realized it was a half-ass recovery really. I was physically a little better, and I learned a little about appreciating life, but this was not the total transformation that happened the second time. There were more lessons to be learned. I can see that now.

DAYS 9-10 TIME IS YOUR CREATION

The next two days of my meditation experience focused on my beliefs about time and being in the "flow" of life. Being in the flow was not something I ever did. Ever. I was always projecting into the future, good or bad. I wanted to control the future as much as possible. But we cannot control the future. I needed to learn to accept how my life was going. This didn't mean I shouldn't go after what I want and make changes—it just meant I needed to learn how to be in the flow and not fight it.

I also needed to learn how to be open and aware. Deepak says we should "renew and refresh with meditation." And not only meditation, but using our time more creatively in ways that will give us a little boost or refresh. I made a list of ways I would use my time creatively and give myself a little refreshing in small ways.

- Dress with more fun in mind.

- Meditate.

- Join an exercise class.

- Learn to sketch.

Dressing with more fun in mind was an easy way to give myself a boost! I have always *loved* clothes. I love shopping in my own closet and putting outfits together! But now I wanted to change things up a little. I started wearing more mixed prints, I bought clothes in brighter colors, I mixed brighter colors, and I bought a pair of leopard print shoes! I started getting a few more compliments, so I kept it up. It's fun, it's a happiness boost and it's easy to do. Win, win, win.

Second on my list was meditate. That's a standard that is always there. Third on the list was joining an exercise class. This wasn't new either, but it made sense to add it to this list because it was an extremely refreshing way to use my time.

Learning to sketch came last on this list. For years I wanted to learn to sketch, mostly because I wanted to sketch the birds I saw at my feeders, but also just because it sounded fun. I bought a simple sketching instruction book and all the supplies I needed. I was so excited! I was learning something new and being crafty! I started off strong, but after a month or so I lost interest. I just didn't have the passion and I wasn't enjoying it. I decided to let this one go. I still would like to learn how to sketch birds. I think that's what I really wanted to do after all, not learn how to sketch everything. What I want to do is very specific. A goal for a future date!

In addition to listing what I wanted to do with my time, I wrote one thing I wanted to stop using my time for, and that was negative friendships. Friends with negative energy bring me down considerably. I'm hyperaware of everyone's energy now. I have done so much work to keep myself in the most positive environment possible that when a negative presence arrives I immediately want to get away. I had to let certain people in my life go because of their negativity. I just can't and don't want to surround myself with that energy anymore. It's tougher with family, but I heard a little tip one day that you should create an invisible force field around yourself so none of their energy gets to you. I love that visualization. It's not easy, but

I can practice no matter whether I'm at work, with family or at an event. I can't control others. I can only control my response. I refuse to let someone else's negativity ruin my state of mind anymore! Are you in control of your time? Are you using your time to refresh? Try the following:

- List three or four ways you would like to use your time to give yourself a happiness boost or a refresh.

- List any ways your time is being taken for nonproductive uses or negativity.

- Follow through to make these changes in your life!

DAY 11 TIME MAKES RELATIONSHIPS BLOSSOM

Day 11's meditation was all about giving relationships quality time. If we don't pay attention to our relationships, they devolve. It's really our choice whether to give our relationships the attention they deserve. I had two issues here. First, I neglected all my relationships (with the exception of my relationships with my mother and my children) during the time I was out of commission. I didn't see any of my friends. For one, I couldn't do anything. And I just didn't want to talk about how awful I felt. I just wanted to feel normal. My relationship with my husband was strained, to say the least. He took on all the driving duties for our kids at this time. My son was about a year away from learning to drive, and when he did that eased up the responsibilities. I couldn't even do the dishes or any housework whatsoever. My husband did what he could, but he was very busy at work. My mom helped out and I ordered my groceries online. My life had come to a halt. That is going to strain any relationship. My husband was feeling the stress of "Why aren't you getting better?" too.

The second issue, and one I cover in much more depth later, is I wasn't great at paying attention to my friendships in the first place. I didn't make friends a priority. I let time slide between seeing them. I would decline invitations for no good reason. I really don't know why I did that, but looking back, it is most definitely a pattern I see.

I've since made my friendships a huge priority. I wrote earlier about the types of people I'm surrounding myself with and about finding my tribe, but what happens when you have your tribe? I began to make those people in my life a priority. I make a point to invite friends to lunch or dinner dates. If I see that I don't have any lunch or dinner dates booked, I start reaching out and getting things on my calendar. I ask myself who I haven't seen in a while or who I need to connect with right now.

I also make sure I'm showing up for friends when needed. I'm quick to offer help now, where, to be honest, I wasn't before. I'm not proud of this. It's just a fact. Now I'm giving. When I am with my friends, I make sure it's a real conversation. And that just comes naturally now because of the people I've surrounded myself with. Taking time to talk is so important. Even just a quick text makes a difference. Are you looking to make your relationships a priority? Try the following:

- Make time to meet up with your friends, whether that means lunch, dinner, a movie or a festival—whatever you enjoy! And make sure you have these dates in your calendar to make them a priority!

- Check in with your friends often just to see how they are doing or even send a quick text to keep connected.

DAY 12 MY TIME, YOUR TIME, AND OUR TIME

According to Deepak Chopra, we all have our own rhythm. We can't and shouldn't expect others to be in our personal rhythm. The ego tells us our time is better, but we do need to respect each other's styles. And when we come together those differences go away and the attention needs to be on "us," not "me." In my notebook I listed three things under My Time:

- Sketching.

- Reading.

- Meditating.

Well, we know what happened with sketching. My intentions were good. I tried it and it didn't stick. That's okay.

Reading is a mainstay in my life and a *big* priority. It gets *a lot* of my free time because I get so much happiness from reading and everything to do with it: browsing the library, reading book reviews, going to author talks and book signings, going to bookstores, talking to others about books—it goes on and on.

The last area I wrote in my notebook under My Time was meditation. Another nonnegotiable. I make sure I have my meditation time early in the morning when no one else is awake and there are no distractions. It's by far my favorite part of my day. I know I'm doing so much good for myself and changing those pathways in my brain!

For Your Time, I couldn't choose what my husband does with his free time. He needs to choose that for himself. Most of the time he will choose golf. He enjoys it because he's in nature, walking and playing a sport he loves. If not golfing, the other activity he chooses for his free time is running.

Then there is Our Time. I've written about this before too—our dates mostly consist of attending concerts and other musical events. We are *big* music people. I didn't realize this until recently. Doesn't everyone want to go to as many concerts as possible? No, they don't actually. Well, these concerts are our dates most of the time. My husband enjoys eating out way more than I do. When restaurants catch up to what healthy eating consists of I will venture out more. A few places are doing it right, but not many. I like knowing what's in my food these days. Do you have scheduled time to yourself? Try the following:

List three or four things you want to do with *your* time.

If you are in a relationship, what could you do or want to do with *our* time?

DAYS 13-14 SEASON OF LIFE

Happy Days = Happy Life. So simple, but so true. Increasing my everyday happiness had become a goal along with everything else I was doing. It also seemed to happen naturally when I started focusing on the things that would help me grow and heal. Like Gretchen Rubin says, I'm living in "an atmosphere of growth."

Deepak asked what three things I was doing in my life that made me happy. That was easy:

- Meditation.

- Exercise.

- Reading.

My mainstays. So what was making me unhappy and stuck in the past (besides the obvious pain issue)? For me, that was worrying about what other people think. And when I say other people, I mean former "friends" whom I considered friends, but it turns out they were not. I had recently made a big change in my life by removing my daughter from her dance studio and enrolling her elsewhere. This may sound like a small thing, but she had been spending more than twenty hours a week in this studio with the same girls and teachers for more than ten years. I became friends with many of the moms as we watched our daughters grow over the years. When we left I assumed I would stay friends with most of them, but that was not the case. It turns out that when you make a change not everyone comes along for the ride. I'm not blaming anyone here. I didn't reach out to them either. It was a huge decision and a big upheaval in my daughter's life. Maybe they didn't know what to say and then said nothing. Uncomfortable feelings occurred on both sides. The easy thing to do is nothing. This unhappiness for me didn't last. I was upset for a time, but I've moved on and realized I have my tribe and I'm all the better for it. Those moms were not my people. A couple of these friends did stick with me and we still see each other often. So after the fallout I was left with the right people and that's the way it should be.

Next I was to look forward into the next five to ten years at what changes were coming in my life and the positive outcomes of those changes. Here's what I wrote:

- Being empty-nesters (good and sad).

- Downsizing.

- Volunteering more.

The idea of being empty nesters is both thrilling and devastating. On the plus side, we will be done paying for college, I will have more time for all the things I enjoy and I won't be locked into the "school schedule" when making plans, among other things. Then there is the obvious sadness that comes when your kids leave. Every time my son comes home from college on break and then leaves, I am sad all over again. I'm so proud of him and excited for his future, but I can't help the tears when he heads out the door.

Downsizing! This is something to get excited about. I can't wait to downsize our home! I'm looking forward to a cozy space, not the oversized house we have now. Don't get me wrong: our house is beautiful and for a time it was functional (although excessive). But this house no longer serves our needs. I'm already giddy about having a smaller mortgage or no mortgage to speak of. It will be life-changing and I can't wait!

The third positive outcome I see is the ability to volunteer more. I'm very happy with my volunteering life right now. I'm heavily involved in a cause I care about deeply. I devote quite a bit of my time to it. But I can see how I will be able to do more and step into other causes I care about in the near future. Have you thought about how you spend your days to make yourself happier? Try the following:

- List three or four things in this current stage of your life that make you happy.

- Ask yourself if something from your past is keeping you stuck and unhappy.

- List three or four things that you see making you happy in the next five to ten years.

DAYS 15-16 MAKING EVERY MOMENT MATTER

Making every moment matter was the focus for this session. Deepak says the present moment is the only real time that exists. Meditation takes you to the "now." I have a much better understanding of this these days, and I no longer let future worries steal time away from me. Being in the flow means I can "feel" my way through life instead of the constant stress and worry.

Here I had to come up with an activity where it felt like time stood still. For me this is being at the beach. I, like many people, find being at the beach incredibly relaxing with the sound of the waves, the hot sun and the feel of the sand. Obviously, I can't be at the beach every day! But the point is to understand the feeling of time standing still when you are in the flow and there is no stress and worry.

On the other hand, now I had to come up with anything that made me feel the pressure of the clock. I had three.

- Getting older.

- Kids' activities.

- Having dinner ready every night.

At the time of this twenty-one-day meditation I really did feel a lot of pressure about my age and where I was in life. I felt like time was short. Part of me was excited to do all these new things, and the other part of me told myself, "Well, it's great you figured all this out, but it's too late to do anything productive with it." I look at that much differently now, partly due to a podcast I absolutely love called *The Sheri and Nancy Show* (formally known as *This Is 50*). You can find it here: https://podcasts.apple.com/us/podcast/the-sheri-nancy-show/id1271868787. At the time of writing this I'm coming up on my fiftieth birthday. The entire idea behind this podcast is that fifty is truly the halfway point. It's about working on all the health and wellness areas in our lives and making the best life we can, and this includes following our dreams and pursuits. This is not the time to slow down or retire as previous generations did. Now is the time to use all your wisdom, focus on yourself and move forward into the next fifty years. This is exactly how I view the rest of my life right now. It's a mindset shift. I'm working on all the areas of my life to make it the best it can be with the goal of another fifty years of health and happiness.

The other two areas of pressure of the clock were not as serious, but still needed to be solved. When my kids were younger, I spent a lot of time getting all their accessories together for whatever activities they were off to. What needed to change was more responsibility on their end in getting all their own belongings together. They certainly were old enough, but honestly I had never asked them to do it before. I took it on when they were little and then never let it go! That changed with me finally telling them it was time for them to take over these duties and with the fact that they were older and actually wanted to do everything on their own.

The third area of time pressure was the never-ending need to have healthy dinners ready for my family. Don't get me wrong: I *love* cooking. And I've also always enjoyed meal planning and grocery shopping. But I was feeling the time crunch every night of getting the meals I had planned onto the table. I didn't solve this issue until recently when I discovered Cassy Joy Garcia's *Cook Once Eat All Week* cookbook. If you follow me on Instagram, you will see all my posts about the dinners I make out of the recipes included in this book! I regularly post about my cooking because I'm genuinely excited about the meals! This book is full of gluten-free and paleo-friendly recipes broken down into weeks with a prep day at the start. The idea is to dedicate a couple of hours to cooking once a week, and then when it comes time to cook the meals for the week you are only assembling and heating the food you have already prepped. It's genius. A lot of meal-planning cookbooks are out there, but *none* of them are paleo friendly and so good! The food is delicious! Much better than most cookbook recipes I've made over the years, paleo or not. And I have an entire collection of cookbooks going back years. Not only am I saving a *ton* of time, I'm also saving *money* because I'm no longer buying five different proteins for the week. I buy one and use it for all the meals for the week in different ways. I can't say enough about it!

DAYS 17-18 - THE WHOLENESS OF TIME

Everything is designed for wholeness, especially in nature. Deepak says not to "measure your life in bits and pieces. The true nature of myself is the wholeness of the universe." Maybe that's a little woo-woo for you. I believe we are all part of something bigger, which in turn makes us feel whole. I feel this way clearly when I'm meditating and when I'm in nature.

Being in nature is a very new thing for me. I've never, ever been outdoorsy. I've only camped a handful of times, most of which were with the Girl Scouts when I was very young and then once in my twenties. It was not my favorite thing to do. I didn't enjoy the bugs, the dirt or the discomfort of being outside. I was a city girl raised in Pittsburgh until I was eleven, then I moved to Southern California and from there to Northern Virginia just outside DC. The only thing I did outside was go to the beach. I loved going to the beach, but not for the reasons I love being in nature now.

Many studies show the health gains for those in contact with nature, which made me take it more seriously. Later it became part of my goals, my vision board and my "18 for 2018" (more to come on that). In my notes from this meditation experience I wrote, "I feel whole when at a park—do more often." That was the beginning, my first thoughts of getting out in nature with purpose. I do this regularly now and *love* it! I have a lot to say on the subject when I write about my vision board for 2018. But for now I'll say I appreciate being outside more than I ever have before in my life. I feel like I've uncovered some sort of secret world in the parks I've been visiting! Of course an entire community of people is in on this world of nature. I'm just a newbie. I feel like a little kid taking pictures of all the creatures and beauty around me. I notice everything now. I'm mindful. How about you? Where do you feel most whole? Try the following:

- List experiences that make you feel whole and present. This could be meditating, hiking, yoga, etc.

- Take a look at your list and pick one or two things to bring into your life more often.

- Your overall happiness will increase when you start seeing yourself as part of the wholeness of the universe.

DAYS 19-21 LESSONS LEARNED

As I came to the end of my first 21 Day Meditation Experience with Deepak Chopra, a few things became crystal clear. For one, transcendental meditation (TM) was amazing and most definitely my favorite form of meditation I had found to date. During those twenty minutes the anxiety and worries melted away. Mantra meditation was for me. Occasionally, depending on the day, I would feel "out of body." It sounds very woo-woo, but it's the best way I can describe the overwhelming calm that came over me. I still do other forms of meditation, but TM will always be my go-to.

A lot of self-discovery went on during these two weeks. The journaling forced me to look at myself and the way I was thinking and behaving in life, and it motivated me to make changes. Or as I would look at myself I could see what I needed to add into myself. Some of my journaling took the form of life goals; some were immediate changes and others led me down the right path.

The most important thing I learned was to focus on staying present. I didn't realize how much I was lost in the future or the past, churning up worries that weren't even real. I was putting my body and my mind through stress that was not needed and that only would cause a fight-or-flight reaction in my brain and body, which I would worry about in it turn. It's a vicious cycle.

This was not the end of my meditation experiences with Deepak Chopra. I went on to do more, and every time I learned more about myself. I could see overlaps with other self-growth programs and goals I had for myself and the journaling I had done in these experiences. You will see in later chapters that I had some real aha moments that made a huge change in the path I pursued. Have you considered meditation? Try the following.

- Download one of the many meditation apps. Popular ones include Insight Timer, Calm, Headspace and 10% Happier. I use Insight Timer, which is free.

- Find a meditation type that works for you. You could try TM, body scans, gratitude, sleep, etc. There are many choices. You could also not do any guided meditation and choose just to have music or nature sounds as your backup. I suggest that if you are brand-new to meditating you try a few short, guided meditations first.

PART 5

SELF DISCOVERY

Mindful Living

MINDFULNESS, CALM AND HAPPINESS

Taking part in Mindful Living Week by the Awake Network was one of the most beneficial things I have ever done for myself. The presenters were top notch and full of useful, practical information and tips that I applied in my life immediately.

Starting on Day 1 with mindfulness, calm and happiness, Dr. Rick Hanson talked about how meditation works in real life. He used the example that when you work out physically it makes you stronger. It's the same with meditation. When you meditate and return to the breath you learn control, and that carries over into your real life. I saw this happen in my own life, which I have written about before. A calm takes over. What a pleasant way to live! It's fascinating to me that every time you get a little lost in meditation then come back to the breath you are having a "mini-awakening," as Dr. Hanson calls it, at that moment. That's so important. The coming back is the brain training. It doesn't matter how many times you get lost, coming back is the exercise. Over time you actually change and thicken the cortex of your brain. You are making structural changes that will impact your life, becoming more empathic and less agitated. This is absolutely true for me. When I heard all of this for the first time I was so excited! I felt like someone had let me in on some sort of secret: that something as simple as meditating could make an enormous change in my brain and body! Dr. Hanson says, "You become what you think about."

If you live in a constant state of worry, as I did for many years, the stress and anxiety is something you not only experience—you become it. This made perfect sense to me as I looked back on the previous year or two. My state of mind was destructive. A state-to-trait if you will, as Dr. Hanson says so well. If you want to learn more, watch the following TED Talk by Dr. Hanson: https://youtu.be/jpuDyGgIeh0. My favorite quote from Dr. Hanson during his presentation was: "What do you want to grow in yourself? Dwell there." Yes, dwell there. *So powerful.* We are growing these muscles for life. And I couldn't wait to get started.

Dr. Hansen also focused on how we need to note the small moments of joy that occur every day and savor and absorb them. There is so much happiness there. Don't let them float by!

Another way to bring joy into our lives is to wish someone else happiness two times a day. This does not need to be said to the other person but can be a personal wish of our own during meditation or when taking a few minutes a day to think about someone else. Wishing someone else was happy automatically makes you happy, according to Dr. Hanson. I agree with this. I did a little experiment with this tip and I found it brought me more happiness. It brought me out of my own head, which is always useful. Think about starting a meditation practice if you haven't already.

- Wish happiness on someone else two times a day!
- Notice the small moments of joy during the day and savor them.

DAY 2 EMBRACE BRAVERY OVER PERFECTION

One of the things I love about learning how to revamp myself and my life is the synergy of it. Every time I started working on one area, it would be reinforced again and again in other programs, teachers, events, books and whatever else I was doing to heal and recover. This workshop was no exception.

On Day 2 I learned about embracing bravery. Perfect! This was my ultimate goal because without it I couldn't get out of my pain cycle. I was all ears. First was a focus on gratitude. We know how powerful gratitude can be. Gratitude calms us, reduces stress and "puts the brakes on scarcity," as the speaker said. The marketing we are bombarded with every day makes us feel like we don't have enough. This skews our thinking and makes us unhappy. The shift to an abundance mentality is key. Gratitude. I learned here not to lie to yourself when writing in your gratitude journal. It must be something you know is the truth because your body will know. I had never thought about this before. Now when I write in my gratitude journal nightly, I make sure I'm honest with myself. Some days are harder than others, but there are *always* five things to be grateful for every single day. This is a game changer to your happiness and attitude. Even when I'm in pain, I can find something to be grateful for.

On to bravery. Bravery is the recognition that things won't be perfect. I love that! I've heard versions of this before, but not put this way. I've also heard that perfectionism is based in fear! That makes a lot of sense, doesn't it? We don't want to be judged. If we make it perfect, no judgment. I'm guilty of this. Or I was. I would avoid doing things for fear of being judged. And now I'm free from that! Like when writing this book! I'm laying it all out there! Some of it is embarrassing, and I'm sure I will be judged by some for what I'm saying or how I'm saying it, but in the end I just want to do what I want to do and follow my path. Being brave. It's new to me and oh so rewarding. I have no idea the outcome of this book or my blog, but I feel the need to do them, so out they go into this world!

Another note from this presentation was that helping others is where you transform and become happy. Our own basic self-care needs to be addressed first. Did you ever see that mom at school volunteering and she's a bit of a mess, running late, kids half-dressed, hasn't eaten, etc., but she's there to help at school. What is she able to give of herself at this time? If she had taken care of herself first, she would be in a much better state of mind and much more productive in her volunteering.

Turning to others and helping is important to our happiness as it gives us meaning and fulfillment. We need to not do what we think we "should" do. We need to think about what is important to us. I did *a lot* of volunteering over the years at my children's schools. I was on the PTA for four years in addition to helping in both kids' classrooms and the school library and special events. All very important. But there were other issues and causes I felt strongly about but did not spend *any* time volunteering for. That came later on, when I figured out what would be the most satisfying and where the need was the greatest. Volunteering and meaningful volunteering are two different things. Clearing that up has been very rewarding for me. Are you looking to start a gratitude practice? Try the following:

- Write down five things you are grateful for every night. Remember to be honest with yourself. Your body will know the truth!

- Don't be a perfectionist! Bravery is the recognition that things won't be perfect.

Find volunteer opportunities that are meaningful to you. Do what's meaningful, not what you think you "should" do.

DAY 3 CHANGE YOUR BRAIN!

The more I learn about neuroplasticity the more excited I get. I'm so fascinated by the fact that we can change the pathways of our brain by changing our behavior. We are learning now that our brains are *not* hardwired and incapable of change. The exact opposite is true. Changing the neural pathways in our brain is key to successful change and growth in ourselves. According to Healthtransformer.com, "Neural pathways, comprised of neurons connected by dendrites, are created in the brain based on our habits and behaviors. As patients participate in new activities, they are training their brains to create new neural pathways. The pathways get stronger with repetition until the behavior is the new normal." New normal! That's what I was shooting for in all the work I was doing on myself. I knew retraining my brain was necessary to heal and get back to a normal life.

Day 3's speaker was Geneen Roth. I highly recommend checking her out if you have not heard of her. Geneen says that "the neural pathways in our brains were established as early as childhood. The feeling of 'I don't matter' as a child takes you into adulthood." Wow. Now, I'm not blaming anyone here. I think we *all* have things about our childhood we would like to change. For the most part I had a normal childhood, but there were a few dark chapters. I'm positive those episodes have stuck with me and were never resolved with counseling of any kind. Traumatic events that happened when I was at the ages between fourteen and twenty-three never were addressed in any way. My family and I just pushed forward and wanted to (understandably) move on and leave all of that behind. Sometimes the result was good, but in the end I had all of these things that happened to me that were never addressed properly. That catches up with you. It caught up with me in the form of panic attacks, excess partying and recklessness, and in my late teens I engaged in some very risky behavior that put me in situations I can't believe happened when I look back. (Those stories could be a whole other book!) Eventually I got my act together, got married and established a wonderful life. But all of that "stuff" was still there. You cannot live through trauma and not have it affect you at some point. I'm not saying this is the root of *all* my issues—according to my mother, I was an anxious kid. But I do know it most likely made an imprint on my nervous system that came out as triggers later on in life. What can be done? Science now tells us meditation changes our brains. Geneen says to practice the following to create new patterns:

1. <u>Come into your body.</u> This is just being aware of your body. Have you ever done a mindful body scan meditation? I actually think it is the best type of meditation if you are dealing with stress or anxiety.

2. <u>Turn toward what seems challenging. Don't push it away—go deeper. Don't be frightened of the feelings.</u> My mantra! Feel the fear and do it anyway! This just keeps coming up over and over again, everywhere. It's *so powerful.*

3. <u>Disengage from blaming in the head. Don't judge.</u> Stop the blame game.

4. <u>What's not wrong?</u> This was a game changer for me! I already had a gratitude practice, but to actually sit down and ask this question before writing in my journal was huge! Asking what's not wrong makes you focus on exactly what you are grateful for! Try it!

Try some of these strategies in your own life, whether it's a mindful body scan meditation, a gratitude practice, feeling the fear and doing it anyway or practicing stopping the blame game in your own head.

DAY 4 YOUR ENVIRONMENT MATTERS

Refuge: a condition of being safe or sheltered from pursuit, danger or trouble. Day 4 of the mindfulness challenge covered creating an environment that is both positive and inspiring. This includes your physical space, the activities you participate in, the people you surround yourself with and your social media. There was a lot for me to learn here, and some reinforced what I was already working on.

First, where is your refuge? For me, it is most definitely home. This is my space to recharge my batteries. Being out in the world "doing" requires time to recharge. Being with people and "doing" is the *most* energizing thing for me, yet I resist it. My new attitude of saying yes as often as possible made this abundantly clear. As much as my social life was giving me energy, I also need time to recharge. And I need my environment to be a place of inspiration and calm. This also falls under the change I made regarding improving my home life. Small things can make a big difference. Cleaning something or removing clutter can bring instant calm and happiness.

This presentation reminded me of Gretchen Rubin's book *Outer Order, Inner Calm*. A fabulous read! Clutter creates anxiety and I certainly didn't need any more of that in my life! The goal for me was to do small things daily to boost this sense of calm and happiness. Here are examples of some of the changes I made.

- Keeping the sink clear of dirty dishes.
- Filing away all papers and mail as I open them.
- Taking the trash out immediately.
- Making my bed every morning.

Your environment also includes any activities you are involved in. Trying something new creates all kinds of benefits like thickening the cortex of our brains. The goal here was to find an activity that brought me happiness, that I found interesting and that was satisfying to my soul. I decided yoga would be my thing. I had practiced yoga on my own at home, probably doing the poses all wrong. In fact, I know I was. But at the time I was not a "class" exercise person. After discovering the importance of group exercise with an educated trainer, I was off and ready to try new things. I love yoga. My first class was a free outdoor class, which checked a few boxes for me: it was a form of outdoor exercise, it was a group setting, it was with a skilled instructor and it was a form of exercise and meditation. How could I not go? I'm thankful to a friend of mine who suggested this class. It got the ball rolling for exercise outside of the safe zone of my therapy and fitness center, which had to happen eventually. I needed to see what I could do out in the world. First of all, yoga, real yoga, is hard. Let's make that clear. I was not the best at yoga in the beginning. But I loved that I could do it, modified in the beginning, and I was learning correct form, which is the most important thing in the end. I did those classes once a week for an entire summer then signed up for a membership at the studio that had offered the summer program. I fell in love with this studio and its instructors immediately. These classes were a little harder, but I felt safe there. It was painful at times. I had to call on my practice of "exposing myself slowly," telling my body this is the new normal and to get used to it. It took a long time, and after about a year of doing yoga three or four times a week, I have seen huge progress. So much tension has left my body. Yoga provides two other benefits that were important to what I am trying to achieve in my life. One, mentioned here on Day 4, was learning something new. I had to concentrate on what the instructor was saying. I was learning new poses and positions for seventy-five minutes. Mindfulness is a *must*! It was serious brain retraining! The other was the meditative side of a yoga class. When you are holding a pose you have to stay mindful to maintain it. Outside distractions slip away. Every class ends with Savasana, a total relaxation pose. Sometimes the instructor reads a poem, other times the instructor plays quiet music, but I always feel transported during this time in class. My body is wiped out, completely exhausted, it's hot, I'm extremely sweaty and now I'm just lying there taking it all in. It's gratifying. It's hard to explain how much I love it.

Your virtual environment is also important, I learned. I didn't take this action seriously until about a year after I did this workshop. Recently I did a digital declutter, which I write about in later chapters, but at this point in my life I was wasn't ready to hear it or do it, so I made small changes like changing my home screen to something inspiring, I deleted a few apps to declutter my phone's home screen and I narrowed down pages on my Facebook feed. These were all positive changes, but the big digital declutter came later.

And then came human connection. I learned about tribes and how our social connection is the key to happiness and longevity. Even though I wrote about my tribe earlier, like I said, that was something that just happened, and I realized later I was building my tribe without knowing it. Tribes make us feel safe, reduce stress and bring us joy! One of the actions suggested here, which I did immediately, was to "curate your social circle"—to list the people you see most often and weed out (I know that sounds harsh) who you want to keep in your circle. We need to keep positive energy flowing around us. If we surround ourselves with negative people, they will drag us down and zap our energy. Finding inspiring people became a goal. In my notebook I wrote the following:

- Meetups.

- Volunteer.

- Environment.

All of these became a focus for me over the next year. And I still am always on the hunt. I recently discovered hiking. It's a new passion of mine. I'm in the process of researching hiking groups, but at the same time I've been enjoying hiking with my husband on Sundays. My plan is to keep that up, but also to find a group of ladies to hike with during the week when I have time. Like yoga, this will give me social connection, exercise outside, connection with nature and mindfulness. How can you change your environment to be more positive and inspiring? Try the following:

- Clean something.

- Remove clutter.

- Try something new (maybe a class).

- Thin out your social media feed to what inspires and uplifts.

- Curate your tribe. List of the people you surround yourself most often and decide who stays and who goes to keep positive energy around you. Find new groups and volunteer opportunities that fit your goals.

DAY 5 SPIRITUAL FRIENDSHIPS

The last day of my mindfulness workshop was all about relation-ships, specifically friendships and romantic relationships. This concept is similar to building your tribe but is more focused on pursuing the rela-tionships and friendships you want in your life. Because of this idea, I notice I'm always "on alert" when meeting new people. I'm looking for signs that we have similarities. It could be social justice or mindfulness or one of many things. I recently met a woman at work who I connected with instantly, not because I knew so much about her, but because she matched my energy, which is rare. I feel like I have a ton of energy, I talk a lot and I'm a doer. So when I find someone who speaks animatedly like I do, I'm drawn to them like a moth to a flame! After talking for only a few minutes, we exchanged contact information. I don't see her at work often, but when I do we greet each other with hugs and begin talking so much we lose track of what else is going on around us. This is a spiritual friendship. Another lightening bolt friendship happened while I was attending an event for an organization I volunteer with. I got to talking to a woman I've only talked to in passing once or twice. Again, she matched my energy immediately, but this time it turns out we are incredibly alike, maybe more alike than any other friend I've made in many, many years. We became good friends shortly after! These are the people to surround yourself with. I'm aware I cannot and should not be pushy. Friendships either happen or they don't, but engaging is key. You will not curate your tribe if you don't get out there and meet people and then talk to them with meaning. What I do now that I never would have done before is to invite people I've met to get together as soon as I see or hear of something I know they would be interested in. Or just lunch, as soon as possible! I can't tell you how rewarding this is. These kinds of friendships are different from the friends you make because you have kids on the same sports team or in the same classroom. Maybe that's all you have in common! The question to ask yourself is, "Who do I want to bring into my life as a friend who shares similar values?" Life changing.

I'm not expert on romance or intimacy, but there were a few nuggets to take in here. The idea is that most couples feel disconnected in some way and they want to be closer. We are connected but separate. If you want more connection, you have to act that way. There's a revelation! Gretchen Rubin says, "Act the way you want to feel." This really works. If you haven't tried it, I say give it a go. It's kind of like "fake it 'til you make it." Eventually you will catch up to feel like what you were doing to fake it. Other take-aways I found helpful were the following.

- Precision: Pay attention to the other person. Have good manners. Be thoughtful and honest.

- Openness: Equal importance is given to you and the other person.

- Romance: Romance ends. But you can increase intimacy. It has no end.

I have to say these are all works in progress for me. I've been married to a great guy for twenty-four years, and in that time I may have lapsed on a couple of these, to say the least. I also think the fact that our kids are older now and we can start spending some time away together resolves a lot of these issues. We can now plan a hike or movie without thinking about who am I driving where today. The kids can now drive themselves! My life is not their life anymore. In some ways, that makes me want to cry! On the other hand, life is changing and our relationship is changing too. And that's a good thing. Have you built spiritual friendships? Do you want to connect in your romantic relationships? Try the following:

- Seek out friendships with people with similar values who enjoy the things you enjoy and align yourself with those people.

- Take the initiative to meet up with these new friends. Don't wait!

- In your romantic relationships, try paying attention to the other person, being honest and being thoughtful.

NAMING MY NEW CHAPTER

After completing my second Happiness Project, I spent some time listening to Mel Robbins. Mel Robbins is a motivational speaker who recently started her own talk show. I found her when she was interviewed on one of my favorite podcasts. A lot of what she said resonated with me and put some things about my life into perspective.

When I thought about what I wanted my life to look like two or three years ahead as she suggests, I envisioned the following:

- A job with meaning and purpose.

- Positive, uplifting friends.

- Activity without pain.

- Freedom from money worries.

- Activism.

- Increased reading.

- Mindfulness and optimism.

These were big-picture goals. Now it was about taking the steps to align myself with that vision. If I've learned nothing else, I've learned *action* is key to every single change you want to make in your life. Period. The end. You can put up slogans and quotes all day, but there is no meaning behind them without the work. I see the difference. I would read quotes like "Be yourself" and think *That's nice, yes, be yourself.* But now it screams at me! Be authentic! Fill your life with what makes you happy! When you are actually feeling the affects of taking action, a statement like "Be yourself" becomes extremely powerful and a huge motivator. These were my new eyes through which I was looking at the world.

Mel also talks about using our problems as excuses to not take responsibility. Guilty, guilty, guilty. I could hear all the "I can'ts" coming out of my mouth over the years. She suggests naming the old chapter in your life and then naming the new chapter in your life. I decided to call my old chapter "Fearful, Self-Centered Mona" and my new chapter "Giving, Loving, Brave Mona." That sums it up nicely! It was a clear way to see how I was behaving and how I wanted to live going forward.

I decided to live in a "growth mindset" from then on. I had a past full of bad experiences that had brought me to where I was, and in a lot of ways I'm thankful for all the trauma I'd been through recently because if I hadn't gone through that, I would not have tackled all these other areas in my life. My "why" was abundantly clear. I would have continued letting things happen to me instead of taking control. Mel explains our mindset is fixed in childhood. I've addressed some of the issues of my childhood and their impact on me. Mel woke me up to the fact that I could be repeating negative self-talk all the way back to childhood. Looking back on how much I survived, it's possible there's a little posttraumatic stress disorder there. I never thought about these episodes carrying over to my adult life, but they certainly do. How many adults are part of the walking wounded, without any resolution? If you want to learn more about Mel Robbins, you can find her at melrobbins.com. Do you have a name for an old chapter of your life? How about your new chapter?

THE FOUR TENDENCIES

I can't tell you how much self-knowledge has changed my life. It makes everything much clearer and easier. Knowing yourself enables you to pursue all those things in life you want to pursue; it allows you to tackle problems and make changes. One of the ways to do this is to know your tendency, as Gretchen Rubin lays out in her book *The Four Tendencies*. This is just one small slice of your personality, but an important one. Your tendency shows how you respond to expectations, both inner and outer. Gretchen categorizes the tendencies into the following groups: Upholders, Questioners, Obligers and Rebels.

I'll start with the Upholder tendency because I fall into this category! Upholders easily meet inner and outer expectations. They like to-do lists and generally can do what is it is they want to get done. They are doers and rule followers. On the downside, they can be rigid and can seem like a killjoy. They also experience "tightening," which is when they go beyond the rules to make more rules. They can be told they have a "extreme personality" (I've been told that). I tip a little bit to Questioner, but not much. This is the second smallest group of the four.

Questioners only meet expectations that fit their criteria. If they believe it to be true or from an authority they trust, they will meet the expectation. Everything becomes an inner expectation. They tend to analyze to death and have difficulty making a decision. They can end up in "analysis paralysis." Questioners also don't like to be questioned. I can vouch for all of this, as my husband is a Questioner.

Obligers are the largest group! Most people are Obligers. They meet outer expectations but have trouble meeting inner expectations. They can meet the work deadline, but have trouble sticking to their exercise program. Obligers do well with an accountability partner. They will meet the expectation if someone else is expecting it from them. Accountability partners or accountability in some form are key for Obligers.

Rebels are the smallest group. Rebels only do what they want to do. They tend to not meet inner or outer expectations unless they want to. If someone tells them to do something, it makes them not want to do it more. Rebels do not like to-do lists. Reframing the situation usually works well for Rebels. Forming the expectation into something they want for themselves is key.

Not only is self-knowledge important, it's also helpful in all of your relationships. Now that I know my husband is a Questioner, I can see when his tendency is showing immediately and most of the time it doesn't get under my skin because I take a moment to pause and remind myself his Questioner personality is coming through. I think it helps with friends, families and coworkers as well. Once you know the structure, it's pretty easy to identify someone's tendency, and therefore you can more easily understand where they are coming from. If you want to know your tendency you can take the quiz on Gretchen Rubin's website: www.gretchenrubin.com.

PART 6

AWAKENING CONTINUED

21 Day Meditation Experience Round 2

DESIRE

Now it was time for another 21 Day Meditation Experience with Deepak Chopra! This time the topic was desire and manifestation. Deepak explained that, very much like the law of attraction, we are always sending out vibrations of energy and what we put out comes back to us. Always. Like attracts like and you attract who you are! So if you change your intention, you change your path. Life-changing information here. He went on to say that our inner intentions lead to outer results. Our thoughts are powerful!

Before I get into what I learned in this lesson, let me point out this particular experience was life changing for me. I found so much self-discovery in these lessons. Every day I was inching closer to what I wanted and the path to get there was coming into focus. When I look back at my notes I now can see this is where so much of my future began. Here we go.

I first made a list of my hopes and desires for the 21 Day Meditation Experience. Here was my list in the summer of 2018.

- To be less fearful (conquer fears).

- To go after what I want.

- To be kind and giving and mean it.

- To find part-time work that works with my health priorities.

- To go back to school in some form.

- To be as pain free as possible.

Reading this list now makes me emotional. I completed all of these things. It took a lot of work, but I've said it before and I'll say it again—action steps are the key. If you don't take action, nothing will happen. Putting out the energy I want to receive works. If you don't believe me, give it a try. I think you will be surprised!

Next I listed my daily desires.

- Love (being kind to others).

- Alone time (just what is needed).

- Connection and friendship (say yes and be open).

- Rest.

- Improvement of my home life.

- Planning (don't overdo it).

I had to be careful with alone time and planning because I could do that all day, and I have. Planning, planning, planning, by myself, for hours. That's my Upholder personality on steroids. I need both of those things in my life, but now I'm aware of the trap of falling too deep and getting carried away into my default behavior. Being self-aware always allows me to see my personality traits in action and put a stop to it when I need to, especially when I know it's not going to benefit me and could possibly be a negative in my life.

Take a minute and think about your hopes and desires. Then make a list to remind yourself of what you want your life to look like. Next, begin to act the way you want to feel. I've heard Gretchen Rubin say this too, and it also applies to the law of attraction. Attract the energy you want to receive. Remember—like attracts like!

DAY 2 FEELING ALIVE!

On Day 2 Deepak told us desire is natural and creative. Fulfilling your desires is to fulfill your intentions. He said something here that struck me: "Plan your life around desire." That sounded a bit selfish to me at first, but when you think about it, it's not. Life would be so much less interesting without any desires! Deepak explains the highest desire is to grow and evolve. I like to think I live in a "growth mindset" or, as Gretchen Rubin says, "live in an atmosphere of growth." When we think about desire this way, it makes more sense to plan your life around your desires.

If I didn't have the desire to heal and recover from my back and neck issues, I would have never met such an incredible group of women. And I never would have had that positive support system to carry me along. If I didn't have interests or passions, I never would have returned to my book club after missing out for so long. My love of books and the desire to see my old friends opened me up to books I wouldn't have chosen on my own.

All of these small desires make life better. If nothing else, the past two or three years has taught me that going after and pursing those desires is incredibly important. All the actions I took made huge, sweeping changes in my life that made me significantly happier, calmer and healthier. Without desire, where would I have been?

Ask yourself what your life would look like without desires, interests or passions! I think we all know how that would make us feel, but it's a good exercise to go through to remind us what makes us feel alive!

DAY 3 MANIFESTATION

Today's lesson was all about getting closer to your true self, which we can achieve in meditation. Deepak says when we get closer to our true selves we can attract our desires into our life and to let our soul be our guide. This reminded me of an interview I heard on a podcast where the discussion was all about soul writing. Soul writing is when you spend time in a quiet space writing in free form. Whatever comes to mind, you fill the page with it. I've heard people say some of their best ideas come from this form of writing. I have to admit this has been on my to-do list for at least a year. My plan is for it to go on my 2020 vision board!

My notes from Day 3 are telling of my state of mind at the time. I could not see things manifesting in my life. I think that was the universe telling me to get my priorities in order, which does happen with a little more work. Here are my notes from this lesson.

QUESTION 1

Name three things you wish you could have in your life and believe to be unattainable, so much so that you resigned yourself to not having them.

My answers are so telling here.

1. To be pain free.

2. To not be afraid of the medical community.

3. To redecorate the house. (SIDE NOTE: I still can't believe with all I had going on that I listed this as a "wish," but there is it. I'm not editing, but being honest in all its glory!)

QUESTION 2

Reasons why they will not manifest.

1. Too much damage to my body.

2. I don't know how to begin to trust doctors again.

3. Not enough money.

QUESTION 3

Ways nature could arrange for me to get my desires. (Imagine it!)

1. Yoga works. I get injections. I continue physical therapy. My brain settles down.

2. Work on ABCDE problem-solving. Dispute my thoughts. Keep working on coping skills.

3. I get a part-time job.

When I wrote I wanted to be pain free, it felt like a wish and not at all attainable. But when I read my answer on how to get what I desire, I was on the right track, even then. This just proves to me that the law of attraction works and was working in my life. Yoga has been a *huge* healer. Yoga gives me strength and flexibility, relieves my muscle tension, reduces my stress and forces me to practice mindfulness. It's the best part of my day, for sure. Problem-solving is another key and something I've written about already here. I needed to keep up this strategy in my life if I was going to make it happen.

Part-time work! Yes, after twenty years as a stay-at-home mom I finally came to the realization that if my husband and I were going to send our kids off to college debt free (meaning them *and* us), then more money needed to come into the house in addition to budgeting and getting a hold of our personal finances. Again, a huge stress reliever! Later in this program I discovered what I wanted as I got in touch with my true self. Spoiler alert: I am working a part-time job now, but I'll save the details for a little later. Think about your desires and go through these questions. I think it can be a very eye-opening exercise!

DAY 4 I JUST HAVE JET LAG

Here's something I know to be true. When you want something to happen in your life, instead of worry and anxiety taking over, you let it go. Deepak says when you become detached you become open to whatever happens. This was a big lesson for me. I liked to control everything that happened to me as much as possible. This way of living causes so much stress, and we all know what stress does to the body. I can see how much more I'm in the flow now. But, even before I learned this lesson, there was a time in my life when this was working in my life and was crystal clear.

When my husband and I decided to start a family we thought once I went off the pill, I would immediately get pregnant. Isn't that why I took the pill for so long? Because it's so easy to get pregnant! Well, that was not the case for us. Month after month, nothing. My OB-GYN had me charting and taking my temperature and taking medications to help the process along. But after many months she sat us down and told us she'd done all she could and was referring us to a fertility specialist. I was shocked. Why couldn't I get pregnant? We moved forward and made an appointment with the specialist. In the meantime, I decided to let it go. I could not let it consume me. Shortly before my scheduled appointment with the fertility doctor my husband and I took a trip to Colorado for a family reunion. When we got back and I returned to work, I felt tired. Really tired. I was fighting to keep my eyes open while driving home from work. I thought *Wow, this is some serious jet lag I have!* On day two of feeling this way, I mentioned to my girlfriend at work how I was feeling. She knew about my fertility issues and said, "Maybe you're pregnant." I did not even consider this a possibility. But I had still been taking my medication and doing all my tracking, so that day I bought a pregnancy test. My husband was home, chatting on the phone with his brother, when I slipped away to take the test. And there it was. I was pregnant! I didn't even wait for my husband to hang up the phone! I just yelled out, "I'm pregnant!" which he told his brother, and the news was out!

I truly believe the act of letting go helped tremendously in getting pregnant. I left it up to the universe and the universe responded. Once the worry and the need for control were gone, things happened the way they were supposed to. Have you ever had a moment in your life when you let go? What was the outcome?

DAY 5 MY TRUE SELF

Today's lesson was about exploring who you are and the reasons we feel the desire for more. More food, more distractions, more money. Just more. Why do we feel we are lacking? Deepak say our true selves are whole and if we just "be ourselves," the energy of attraction will be enough.

Now we are getting into the nitty-gritty. I had to look at myself and ask, "How do I feel unworthy?" And my answer was gut-wrenching: I'm not smart enough to go back to school. That's hard to say and even scarier to write. But I'm being totally honest, so, here we go. Because of my family situation at the time, I did not have the opportunity to finish college. My parents were separating and I went to live with my mom, which meant kicking in for rent. I started going to school at night and working full-time during the day. Even after I left that situation, I never went back to school full-time. I continued working and going to school. I thought I would get done eventually. Fast-forward to when I started dating my husband. We knew from when we were dating that we both wanted kids and that I would stay home with them. It was a shared value. My husband was also going to school at night, and we were both paying our own way. The plan was that we would pay for him to finish school, get married and I would quit school because I was going to stay home with our future children. This is a twenty-something mentality. I would love to tell my younger self how important it is to finish school! This would hang over my head as a regret that I carried the rest of my life. Not because the degree is so important. It's not really. It's the sense of accomplishment. I should have finished. I've learned to let that go and move on. But that unworthiness was there. I could feel it. This is when I started pondering going back to school in some form. I couldn't do exactly what I wanted to do, which was public health. I couldn't at the time because, as I explained earlier, our money was budgeted for college for our children, so I could not justify a four-year degree for myself. I decided getting my certification as a health coach would be perfect for now. The other dream is not gone!

The next question was, when did I feel successful? Two things came to mind. One was that between my two health episodes I started selling cosmetics. And surprise! I was good at it. I was always the top representative on our team. I had no idea I could sell until I tried!

The second thing that came to mind was that in my exercise classes with Carrie I felt like anything was possible. There were *no* restrictions on what I was capable of, and I felt incredibly strong. This carried over into other areas of my life. I could see my behavior changing. I found a combination of strength and confidence from Carrie and calm from my meditation. It was serving me well.

Now I was to make a list of words that described my true self. Here we go:

successful
joyful
strong
energetic
leader
powerful
confident

These are words that others have used to describe me and that I feel are at the core of who I am. What a great exercise in self-knowledge this was! Ask yourself these deep questions. How do you feel unworthy? When did you feel successful? Then make a list of words that describe your true self. Think of what others say are your positive traits.

DAY 6 THE LAW OF ATTRACTION

"What you dwell on is what you receive," according to Deepak Chopra. It was clear to me if I continued to sit around dwelling on how much pain I was in and how I couldn't do the things I used to do, I was just going to attract more of the same. Deepak says our power comes from our attention. This is so true. What we pay attention to does indeed grow. He explains desire needs nourishment in the following ways:

- Have a clear intention (no excuses).

- Have positive emotions.

- Believe it will be beneficial for you.

- Prepare for any response. Be flexible.

- Be confident aid will come from the universe.

What I needed to work on most was to "prepare for any response." I was one who loved to control outcomes. But you really can't control outcomes. All you can control is your reaction to them. I'd been screwing up that part all my life. I no longer do that, or at least I catch myself before the damage is done. I'm so self-aware that I have learned how to be more in the flow. As a reminder, I wear a little rope bracelet with a silver disc engraved with the word FLOW. If you would like to focus your attention to attract the things you want in your life, try these steps to start changing what you dwell on.

DAY 7 DEEP DESIRES

On Day 7 Deepak talked about accessing our deepest desires through meditation. Something about doing the meditation practice and then answering the journaling questions works in getting clear. If I was to just sit down and say to myself, "What are my deepest desires?" I don't think I would get nearly the honest, clear answers I would without meditating first. Remember, meditation brings us closer to our true selves. No ego. This is where it gets real.

First I had to list two desires for companionship. Mine were:

- A true best friend and confidant.

- An improved marriage.

Fortunately, I have a lot of friends. But I was narrowing my tribe down to the people whose energy was in sync with mine, people who were supportive and uplifting. But down deep I wanted a true best friend. Someone I could call at all hours, cry my heart out to, laugh with and be completely authentic. I have bits of that in my friendships now, but I would love a couple of really close girlfriends in my life! I'm always working on bringing this into my life by having intention, using life visioning and being open and in the flow. I know it will come—it's just a matter of when!

I think everyone wants to improve their relationship with their spouse. This is more complicated than friendships. I've learned over the past few years you just can't change other people's behaviors. You can only change your own behavior and hope you lead by example. I've seen this work in many ways in my life. I need a constant reminder of this because we get so comfortable in marriages and our spouses tend to bear the load of our worst selves. It's always a work in progress!

Second, I was to list two career desires. Mine were as follows:

- Find a meaningful part-time job in the health/wellness field or volunteer organization.

- To have my own success.

When I wrote down these career desires, having a part-time job seemed like just a hint of an idea. I hadn't worked in twenty years, and the thought was jarring. *What will I do? Am I capable? Where will I work? Will anyone hire me?* This was before I decided to get my health coaching certification. It all came together a few months later when I got very clear on my future goals. This was a first step to realizing I wanted to be in the holistic health and wellness space in some form. And as far as having my own success, I really hadn't up to this point. I hadn't ever set goals for myself. It's hard to have success without goals! I wanted to see what I was capable of. I had big dreams now and goals in place to get there. Just putting this out into the world, I have seen the right people show up in my life at the right time to help me achieve those goals. That is the law of attraction in action.

I now have a part-time job at my local library, which checks the meaningful box. And I have my blog and book project for the health and wellness side. So that desire, for now, leads down two different paths.

My last assignment was to list two desires for my health. That was easy. That's how this whole journey started!

- To be pain free.
- To become strong.

This entire journey started with my desire to become pain free. That was the beginning and still is the goal. And getting stronger just goes along with that. It's all wrapped up together. It is a work in progress, but I am so, so close to getting there. The progress I've made over the past two years surprises me when I read my notes. I'm so thankful for all of my journaling during this time. Seeing all my progress and growth in writing is powerful!

What would be my emotional outcome from fulfilling these desires? I wrote:

- Happiness.
- Confidence.
- Well-being.

Who wouldn't want that? Deepak says to be less focused on the details of your desires but to become open to what will happen as new options present themselves. I've learned changes and disruptions that come usually arrive to teach me something. There is always a lesson and an opportunity to grow. Now I see it, whereas before I only ever saw the stress and worry. I suggest diving into your deepest desires. I highly recommend doing a little meditation practice first. This is incredibly helpful in getting in touch with your true self.

DAYS 8-9 GOING DEEP

Days 8 and 9 were focused on going deeper into the mind through awareness and meditation. Deepak explained that (and if you have meditated for any length of time you are aware) whether you are using a mantra or are just focused on the breath, there is a gap where you are not focused on the mantra or the breath because you are in between repeating the mantra in your head or in between breaths. This is where the magic happens. There are no thoughts in the gap. They are little blips of silence, and that is the core of coming in touch with your true self. I absolutely treasure these moments in meditation. It doesn't always happen, as sometimes thoughts come about and you steer yourself back to your mantra/breath. Over and over again. But that is also good because that is how you build muscle memory in your brain. I've heard it compared to working out. It's basically the same thing. Keep building that muscle until it gets stronger. The best part is when this calmness that happens in the gap manifests in your everyday life. I have seen this happen in my own life, and it's something to behold. I'm grateful I have found this practice. No drugs or therapy required!

Next I was to come up with times in my life when I felt in the flow and "close to the source of my existence." That's pretty deep! When I'm near water, especially at the beach, I feel like I've become one with nature. Something about the warm wind, the hot sun, the sand at my feet, the sounds coming from the ocean and the beauty of the ocean itself has that effect on me. It just feels natural. And more recently I have experienced this when hiking. I've occasionally had these peak experiences in yoga where I'm so mindful I truly feel like I'm the only one in the room. I am overcome with calm and peace. I just love it. I routinely put myself in the front row of the studio, even in the beginning, mostly so I can clearly see the teacher. I need to see what is going on. In the beginning it felt like a game of Twister—right hand here, hold left leg, look over right shoulder, left hand in the air—it took a lot of concentration and mindfulness on my part. If you are scattered at all, it will show up in a yoga class. If you miss a cue because your brain is somewhere else, you will be twisting left when everyone else is twisting right. This happened to me over and over again in the beginning. Not only am I getting the physical benefits of yoga, flexibility, strength and improving my nervous system, I'm getting all the benefits of meditation. I can't say enough about it. I suggest, if you are not meditating already, you give it try. Once you get comfortable you may experience the calm in the "gaps" too.

DAYS 10-11 FLOW II

"Everything is as it should be." According to Deepak Chopra, the lessons of Days 10 and 11 were to show that our awareness is flexible and adaptable. I've touched on this before, but let's be clear: I liked controlling situations. Actually, I thought I needed to control situations. The source of much of my stress and anxiety was me fretting over "what's going to happen." Will my kids get on that team? In that class? Get picked in the audition? Letting go of a particular outcome was difficult for me, to say the least. I'm learning to go with the flow and have come so, so far. I know now that whatever the outcome is, it is meant to be. And if I don't get what I want, it's because something better is on its way. I've seen this happen over and over again in my life. Every time something I love comes to an end—a class, an instructor changes when they are teaching, a job, or a particular thing I'm doing becomes too expensive to continue, whatever it is—the outcome of that is always better than the original thing I was doing. It's like the universe is forcing me to change. I wouldn't have made those choices on my own. I was disappointed about those changes, but it turns out some of the best things in my life have come to me as a result of forced changes.

My biggest regret is I did not learn this sooner, especially when my kids were younger. All the time and stress and yelling about things that really weren't important. Who cares if it takes ten minutes for my kids to put on their shoes? I really wish I would have chilled out. I will be the best grandma ever to make up for all of the frustration and anger my kids endured with me. Live and learn.

Deepak explains there are three elements to master for flow. First is flexible consciousness, which is to receive with an open mind. Be open and nonjudgmental. And don't resist. (Don't resist! I should have that hung on a wall in my house or put on my refrigerator so I would see it every day!) Second, go with the flow to arrive at full manifestation. Going with the flow requires practice. Third, remain centered, which comes with meditation practice.

Even in meditation if we let thoughts take over, which of course I have, completely losing the mantra, eventually going back to the mantra means our attention is flexible. It's a good lesson. I'm not striving for perfection; I'm a work in progress. The more self-growth that is happening in my life, the happier and more productive my life becomes. It's incredible to watch. How about you? Are you feeling like you are living in the flow? Take some time to focus your awareness and see if you are being rigid for a particular outcome to happen in your life. What would happen if you started to not resist and had a more open mind about the outcome?

DAY 12 ARE YOUR BELIEFS SERVING YOU?

Living manifestation! I *loved* this lesson. So much to dive into here! Deepak says if we live our lives with anxiety and depression, flow doesn't happen. "If you believe life is stacked against you, you will create an inner conflict." Basically, you get more of what you focus on—the law of attraction. He says we should "choose a lifestyle that is open, low stress, humble, conscious and self aware." I love that. Because I was depressed due to my situation, I had a serious blockage. No way was I sending out the kind of energy that was going to bring me what I truly wanted. I had to choose a lifestyle that reflected what I wanted.

My focus was to make good lifestyle choices going forward. Having intention is so important. So, to get it out of the way because I don't like focusing on the negative, here is what I listed as my bad lifestyle choices at the time:

- Wasting time.

- Spending too much time on my phone.

- Not getting up as early as I should (Getting up late for me is getting up at 7 a.m. To put this in perspective, I now get up at 5 a.m. every day. Occasionally I'll swing thirty minutes one way or the other, depending on the day.)

My good lifestyle choices at the time were the following:

- Eating well.

- Meditating.

- Exercising.

- Reading.

All of these are good choices I continue to this day. They are built into my daily schedule. I make it happen as a part of life now. There is time. You may think you don't have time, but it's amazing what can happen when we cut out or cut down the time killers—for example, TV, phone, sleeping late. The first few hours of my day are so productive. I wouldn't give it up for anything. Are you feeling like some area of your lifestyle is causing a "blockage?" If so, try looking at areas in which you are doing well and what areas you feel like could be causing that blockage. Most importantly, let go of beliefs that are no longer serving you!

DAYS 13-14 AHA MOMENT!

Did you ever have a true aha moment? A true epiphany when you stop in your tracks and are in awe of what is in front of you? This is what happened to me on Day 14. The focus of this particular experience was manifestation. Even the centering thought of the day made me smile: "Fulfilling my dreams fulfills my spirit." Deepak explains fulfilling desires is spiritual. When we allow our desires to become alive, we have a sense of love and joy. When we are in touch with our true selves, we discover who we really are. This awakening happens in meditation. He explains our soul is eager to connect with us.

When I am practicing TM, I sometimes have what I call an outer body experience. I truly "leave" myself. It's incredible. It's not always long lasting, but when it does happen there are no thoughts. This is as close to our true selves as we can get. I believe this is the time to connect with our soul and the best time to listen.

As I went through the journaling for this day, I wrote "Spiritual Values," underlined it, and then wrote the following. "Helping others in my desire to have a career in either health and wellness/advocacy or volunteer field." And second I wrote, "My desire to be pain free will help me and help my family." "Figuring out my true desires. They are evolving as I go through this program. Getting closer to my true self." This was an important moment. My head was so clear from meditation I was forced to dig down and find what I really desired, and that's what I came up with. It was in me and now it was put into words. It set off me off on my path of what was to come. These notes translated into a trip to the library to get the book *What Color Is My Parachute?* which enabled me to further narrow down what I wanted for myself. I started researching holistic health coaching programs, and I started strategizing how to pay for it! Credit cards and loans were off limits. Within a year, I had figured it all out and went back to school and got my certification, which led to a blog and a book. All because I decided to focus on myself in every pillar of my life. And the results are showing. I have one more note I wrote in my notebook on Day 14 with a big star next to it. "The key to the whole program. I figured it out! Decision made!" It makes me smile to read that. Have you given any thought to your deepest desires? I suggest the following. Take some time to meditate to clear your mind and get close to your true self. This takes time. It's not a one-shot deal! Begin to ask yourself what you really want. You will be surprised at what comes out!

DAYS 15-16 DON'T IMPOSE

There is a fine line between helping others and imposing our path onto them. I walk this line all the time because I'm so passionate about what I'm doing and what I've learned. It's the whole reason I write my blog. I suddenly, after never wanting to discuss what happened to me, wanted to scream it from the rooftops to everyone I know. And at first I did. I bombarded my family and friends with "Did you know ... blah, blah, blah?" I'm sure most people heard me saying "everything you're doing is wrong." I get very excited about new things, and the science is there to back it all up, so I felt the need to share. And I'm still doing that. The difference is I'm letting the people who want to know find me instead of telling everyone around me whether they want to hear it or not.

I recently overheard a conversation between two people snacking on peanuts, congratulating themselves on their healthy choice of "nuts" for a snack. Inside I was bursting at the seams. "Peanuts are not nuts, they are legumes, and they are inflammatory! Also, what kind of oil are those cooked in? Most likely canola, which is a processed oil known for causing heart attacks!" My brain was spinning, but I didn't say anything. It's not my place. Deepak says we don't know what another's path entails. We need to let nature take its course. I needed to let go of ego, control and judgment! That resonated with me! As an Upholder (see Gretchen Rubin), I'm programmed to do what is "right" and follow the "rules." So when I read about a way to improve my health and well-being that maybe isn't widely known yet, I just jump aboard and do it. I needed to stop trying to "fix" everyone. On the other hand, helping people is what I'd signed up to do! The difference is when I'm asked, or if it comes up in conversation, I will speak up about what I feel, but I will not jump into a conversation just to tell someone they are wrong. Deepak says we should "envision that everyone's mind/body state is perfect just as they are." That's important to remember. I work on this constantly. Do you try to control others' actions? Are you judgmental? Try reframing these feelings and remind yourself others are on their own path and are right where they need to be. Once we release control, we become more relaxed.

DAY 17 SAY YES TO LIFE!

Day 17 focused on playful manifestation. Deepak talked about "saying yes," which is one of my happiness goals I wrote about earlier. Here I got a much better understanding of why this is so important.

According to Deepak, "to be carefree is to trust the universe to take care of everything." For an Upholder like me this seems like an impossible task. I like controlling situations. "Carefree" was not in my vocabulary. I had spent my whole life up to this point doing the exact opposite. I was never in the flow, always worrying and trying to control outcomes. Desperate and uptight = disappointment. There's a slogan for your fridge! And a good reminder!

Deepak says when we let go of resistance to life it amplifies the law of attraction. I find this to be true. Letting go is a constant struggle for me, although I am *much* improved. For example, as I write this my nineteen-year-old son is planning a four-month-long study abroad trip to Prague. The old me would be sick with worry with all of the possible horrific scenarios worked up and spinning through my head on a daily basis. I would have been losing sleep, researching the area intently and constantly talking it over with my husband. I have done none of that. I'm trusting things will be just fine. If I applied my ABCDE strategies here, I would come to the conclusion that the facts would be on my side and I didn't have much to worry about. That being said, as we get closer to the trip, I will have a talk with my son about safety and we will make sure he has everything he needs. And then I will let go! Life is so much better this way. Both physically and mentally! Are you naturally carefree? Do you aspire to be? Try saying yes to whatever comes your way and see how your life opens up and the law of attraction starts working. Try letting go of controlling outcomes and situations.

DAYS 18-20 KNOW YOURSELF

I'm combining a few days here because some of the work I did was repetitive. These three days were dedicated to connecting with our souls. Deepak says, "We live in grace when we learn to merge the self and soul." And that we are the "captains" of our souls. That's powerful.

Something else he said that really resonated with me was "nothing is happening out of order in your life." We never seem to see these things until we look back with hindsight. Some of the most pivotal moments of my life were either completely unplanned or unexpected. I already discussed my first pregnancy, which was a surprise in a way. I say all the time that everything happens for a reason, and I believe that, even if you don't see the reason right away. Sometimes it takes a couple of months or years before we can look back and realize why things happened in a certain order.

If I hadn't had the shock (and it shouldn't have been a shock) of coming up with all of my son's college tuition money, we still would be living without a budget and making all the same money mistakes we always had. That dire situation forced me to take control of our money once and for all. I can't begin to tell you how different our financial lives are today than they were a year or two ago. I'm always learning, and I actually find personal finance kind of fun now! Who would have guessed? I was the person running away from budgeting in any form because I thought it would limit my spending. But the complete opposite is true. It's incredibly freeing when every dollar is accounted for. Again, sometimes the worst situations bring on the best changes.

Deepak explains when you blossom into who you really are, you can embrace the power of fulfilling your dreams. I love that! I've been blossoming into who I really am for the past two years! And yes, it certainly does come with power. It's all about self perception. There was a time when I thought I couldn't live without alcohol, cheese and sugar, but guess what? I have for years now, and I don't even think about them anymore. And do you know why? Because now I know how much better I feel without any of those things. There is no temptation. Do I want to feel like crap? Or do I want to feel good? Do I want to live a long, healthy life? Or do I want to end up with a host of chronic diseases? Simple really. People tend to think I'm extreme or I'm depriving myself, but it's just knowledge (knowledge plus action). When we all learned what cigarettes do to our health, most people quit. To me, this is the same. I don't smoke for the same reason I don't eat sugar. My health. With the goal of getting to know yourself better, try meditating daily to get closer to your true self. When you are self aware it becomes easier to not only know who you really are, but easier to then start to fulfill those dreams!

DAY 21 LIVE YOUR TRUTH

Last day of my second 21 Day Meditation Experience! And what an experience it was! On this last day Deepak spoke these wise words, which I'm sure you have heard before. "Become the change you want to see in the world."

If I am stressed and angry, then those around me will be as well. And the opposite is also true. If I'm calm and peaceful, then those around me will be too. This is partly emotional contagion, which is real. And its partly that the energy we give and send out into the world comes right back at us (law of attraction). It took me *so long* to figure this out. I can't wait for other people to make me feel the way I want to feel. I have to become what I want to be! Sometimes it's "fake it 'til you make it." Pretending to be confident eventually turns into confidence. I've also realized everyone is winging it! It's true!

I've learned so much in the past few years about myself, my personality traits and how to work with them for a better life, how to eat properly to take care of myself, have goals, etc. So many things. I took charge of my life! Deepak sums it up really well by saying the reason we are here is to "grow, live and prosper." I'll just leave that there. Try one of Deepak's 21 Day Meditation Experiences. They are going on all the time; they are free and easily found on his website.

PART 7

WELLNESS

Wellness Wheel

Somewhere along my journey I ran across the Wellness Wheel. Have you ever seen or worked with one? You can find it here: https://www.unh.edu/health/well/wellness. This wheel sums up what I was trying to do in my life and in a way it is all of health coaching in one place. It basically took all the areas I was working on (and still am) and put them in another format for me to see. I added to my goals by completing this little project.

The categories of the wheel are the following:

- Emotional.

- Environmental.

- Financial.

- Intellectual.

- Occupational.

- Physical.

- Social.

- Spiritual.

The wheel also helped me focus on areas I wanted to bring into my life like environmental work, but I had no real goals yet on how to do that. The wheel is similar to a vision board but much more detailed and more focused on each area of your life. If you listen to *The Sheri and Nancy Show* podcast, you know they focus on some of these areas, calling them "pillars." That works too! They retitled them some, but in the end it's the same idea. I love it. I love anything that gives structure to my goals. My notes in each category are as follows:

EMOTIONAL

- Become an optimist (ABCDE strategies).
- Refute and dispute my own beliefs.
- Become skilled at generating alternatives.
- Problem solve.

FINANCIAL

- Create a budget.
- Pay off all debt.

ENVIRONMENTAL

- Recycle.
- Get involved with the plastic pollution movement.
- Volunteer.

INTELLECTUAL

- Take the Goodreads reading challenge.
- Read every day.

- Listen to audiobooks.

- Learn a craft.

- Take a class.

OCCUPATIONAL

- Find a job with purpose and meaning.

PHYSICAL

- Take strength classes.

- Start massage and physical therapy.

- Try walking, computer, different shoes.

SOCIAL

- Say yes to all invitations.

- Join a book club.

- See my parents often.

- Make lunch dates.

- Visit family.

- Connect with positive people. Keep negativity out.

SPIRITUAL

- Meditate daily.

- Keep a gratitude journal.

- Get outside.

- Attend nature events.

- Garden.

- Avoid multitasking.

This was just the beginning of what I achieved when I started focusing on all these areas. The key was to break them down into little steps and get those actions on my calendar! I would block out time to work on all of them. I love a full calendar. It means I'm working toward everything I want to achieve. If you would like to try using the Wellness Wheel, you can find many blank templates online to help you get started.

NO PREREQUISITES!

I was listening to the *This Is 50* podcast, now called *The Sheri and Nancy Show*, and their guest was a woman named Geneen Roth. She said some things that made me jump-start all I had envisioned for myself.

By this time, I had had the revelation that I wanted to pursue health and wellness in some form but had not acted on it yet. It was brewing. I had a lot of questions and doubts. Was I smart enough? How would I afford school when I was trying to pay for college for both kids? Would it be worth it? Will I have clients? etc. Then, as if on cue, I heard the following about pursuing your dreams:

- Be clear about your wants.

- Believe in your dream.

- Take action.

- Know yourself.

- No prerequisites.

- Increased longevity if you have dreams.

These all hit home with me and were areas I was trying to work on. No prerequisites! That was such a good thing for me to hear! All I did at that point was give myself prerequisites—all the things I thought should be done before I pursued anything for myself such as the kids must be done with college, we need to be debt free, I have to have the perfect business plan. How freeing it was to know I could just start. And that's exactly what

I did. The ball started rolling shortly after this. I like to say it was a "shift." I've had a few of these along the way where I hear or read something that resonates so strongly I make the change immediately. And this was one of those days.

Geneen said "We should ask yourselves.. Who are you now?" That's a really good question because I was no longer the same person I was even a few years ago. Life changes, kids get older, we get older, and we adjust. Or not. And that's when decline happens. This wise person said decline in the body happens when one or more of the following things happens:

- Empty nest.

- Retirement.

- No dreams.

Empty nest was around the corner, I had had no dreams until recently, and retirement was further down the road, but not that far. I decided right then I would not wait until my kids were out of college to pursue my dreams. I would find the funds and the courage to move forward, and that's exactly what I did. Have you put your dreams on hold? Ask yourself why and start taking action on them today. Small steps make big progress.

DISCOVERING AYURVEDA

Learning more about Ayurveda and the *dosha* types is one of my goals for 2020. During my healing journey I touched on it briefly, enough to get me interested. However, at the time I was focused on more dire needs. What I learned was interesting, though. I'm excited to learn more about it in the future!

Ayurveda is a traditional Hindu system of medicine based on the idea of balance in bodily systems and between the mind, body and spirit. It uses diet, herbal treatment and yogic breathing. It's basically the world's oldest holistic healing system. Ayurveda recognizes three main body types—*vata*, *pitta* and *kapha*—which are called *doshas*. First, I took an online quiz to figure out my type. I am *pitta-vata*. From what I determine from the results, I am a two-*dosha* type (which is common). The *pitta* type is more prominent in my mind and the *vata* type is more prominent in my body. Here are the characteristics of each according to chopra.com.

PITTA CHARACTERISTICS (MY MIND TYPE)

- Mind: Sharp, intellectual, direct, precise, discerning.

- Body: Medium build, warm, muscular.

- Skin: Sensitive, prone to acne and flushing.

- Hair: Tendency toward early graying or thinning.

- Appetite: Strong, can eat almost anything, anytime.

- Routine: Precise and organized.

- Temperament: Passionate, ambitious, courageous.

- Conversation style: Speaks to convey a point.

- Shopping style: Spends on luxury items.

- Stress response: Tendency to blame others and ask, "What did you do wrong?"

I relate completely to the *pitta* characteristics on mind, routine (100 percent), temperament, conversation style (to a fault) and stress response (guilty!).

My second strongest *dosha* is the *vata* type.

VATA CHARACTERISTICS (MY BODY TYPE)

- Mind: Quick, creative, imaginative.

- Body: Thin, light frame.

- Skin: Dry.

- Hair: Dry.

- Appetite: Delicate, spontaneous, tendency to skip meals.

- Routine: Variable, spontaneous.

- Temperament: Welcomes new experiences, enthusiastic, friendly, energetic.

- Conversation style: Loves to talk.

- Shopping style: Buy, buy, buy!

- Stress response: Tendency to blame oneself and ask, "What did I do wrong?"

Again I see these characteristics in myself, but this time in my body type. Mostly body (dry skin and hair), temperament (spot on) and shopping style (the old me or if I was to completely let go, this would be my default).

I learned some tips on how to keep myself healthy based on my type. For my *vata* mind type, there a couple of suggestions here I realized I already did and one or two I didn't. Because I tend to be dry, there is a lot of focus on hydration inside and out, taking a bath with essential oils and drinking warm drinks throughout the day. I make a point of doing this now. I've always loved taking baths, but the oil adds a whole other layer to the experience! Also, it was suggested I use oils on my skin, which I haven't done recently. I love essential oils. I haven't dived into them as deeply as I would like to. Not yet!

For my *pitta* mind type the suggestions focused on meditation with intention and waking up early to develop a good routine, both of which I was doing consistently. Where I was falling short was enjoying relaxation with friends and family and leaving "white space" on my calendar. That was a big one. *Pittas* tend to overschedule themselves. I constantly do that. I love a full calendar! Occasionally, though, it will backfire and I'll end up stressed because I overscheduled myself. Leaving some space is a good lesson for me to learn to take that trigger out of my life. Do you want to learn more about Ayurveda? You can go to https://www.webmd.com/balance/ guide/ayurvedic-treatments to learn more. And if you are interested in the *dosha* quiz, head over to chopra.com to find your type!

TOXIC PEOPLE

Toxic people. We all know who they are. They are friends, coworkers and family members. Now that I had learned how to become an optimist, I also needed to learn how to keep negative people out of my life. Some of this is in our control. I can choose my friends. But family members and coworkers are another story. You can absolutely set boundaries with family members. And for the very first time in my life, I did. It's not pleasant, but I've done too much work to let toxicity happen to myself or my family. Remember, emotions are contagious! So choose wisely who you allow into your space. I really don't buy the attitude that just because someone is related by blood you have to spend time with them or forgive all their destructive ways. I choose the people I surround myself with, and that includes family members.

Coworkers are another story. There is no escape! I recently heard Christine Lang's tiny class on *The Sheri and Nancy Show* podcast about how to "cleanse your energy." She says when encountering negative energy to say to yourself, "Please clear me of energy that isn't good." Another strategy, which is the one I try to use, is to visualize yourself in a stream with water running over you and the stream is carrying everything out through your head to your feet. Another visualization she recommends is visualizing yourself going through a car wash, cleansing yourself of bad energy. She suggests using these strategies a couple of times a day as needed. I think these are very helpful in a work situation where you may not have another choice. If you want to learn more about Christine Lang or her "Shielding yourself from negative energy" talk, you can find her here: https://youtu. be/k-w3Ci9m2_k. Do you have toxic people in your life? Think about whether it's in your best interest to keep them in your circle or whether it is better to learn techniques to shield yourself from emotional contagion.

LIVING IN AN ATMOSPHERE OF GROWTH

If I had to describe my journey in two parts, I would say the first part was physical recovery and the second was mental recovery. That's lumping a lot of areas together, but in the end that is what I was doing. One thing truly did lead to another. I would begin a course or hear a talk on a subject I was interested in and it would inevitably send me off in another direction of personal growth. It would have been nice had I decided one day to just start working on all these areas in my life instead of having something so devastating happen to me, but that is not my story. And I think that's true for many people. Unfortunately, it usually takes some horrific event to awaken us to how we should or could be living. To people I'm meeting for the first time, I can seem extreme. This is partially my Upholder personality, which has always been there; it was just focused on other things instead of growth. I live this way because it was a way out of how I was feeling. And I never want to feel that way again. So when someone says to me, "Don't you miss cookies?" the answer is always no. My "why" is crystal clear and keeps me moving forward.

I say all this because the next step in my wellness journey was a class I stumbled upon given by Elisha Goldstein. It was an online mindful living course I did over four or five days. I'm going to share some of the revelations I unearthed while taking this class. You can find out more about Elisha here: https://elishagoldstein.com/.

Did you know our brains are wired to survive, not to be happy? Our brains fear the unknown, so when we try to make changes our brains start to object. It's a survival instinct. When we relax, we calm the nervous system. This jumped out at me because if there was anything I needed to do, it was to relax my nervous system! According to Elisha, the benefits of relaxation are the following:

- Less worry.

- Slower heart rate.

- Boosted memory.

- Better decision-making.

- Less stress eating.

- Protection of mental health.

- Protection of the brain.

All super important. Why would I not want all of these benefits? Sign me up! One of the tips he suggests, which I have used in my own life, is recognizing when you tense up. Around which people or at what time of day does this happen? When it happens, we should breathe and stretch to relax. The Insight Timer app has many one-minute meditations for exactly this purpose. If you are bracing, you need an antidote!

Another tip was to practice single tasking. I've written before about the fact that there is no such thing as multitasking—you are just doing two or more tasks more poorly than you would have if you were doing one at a time. The biggest change in single tasking came with my walks. A couple of times a week I walk at our local nature preserve. I'm fortunate to have this beautiful piece of nature in my neighborhood. When I walk, I do nothing else. I don't listen to anything: no audiobooks, no podcasts, no music. I love all three of those things, but my focus is on the world around me when I am walking. I do some *great* thinking during these walks. Decisions get made because my brain can relax and wander. My decisions to write a book, start a blog and take a part-time job all came out of these walks. Think about if you find yourself "bracing" and what you can do when that happens. Try relaxing by breathing, meditating or stretching. Also try single-tasking. See if it makes a difference. It did for me!

EMOTIONAL CONTAGION IS REAL

Have you ever felt drained after meeting with a friend? Our friends should give us energy, not deplete us. Emotions are contagious. You can learn more about emotional contagion here: https://www.psychologytoday.com/us/articles/201906/protect-yourself-emotional-contagion. That is reason alone to review who you are spending your time with since we are the average of the five people we spend the most time with. Elisha Goldstein explains we are a highly social species, and who we are around influences our behavior. Having a high social connection has become one of my overarching goals for many reasons that I've written about previously, including longevity. I've made huge improvements on this front, but still have more to work on.

In this lesson I was to list the people I spend the most time with and then rate them on a scale of one to ten by asking how much that person inspired me. At the time I came up with a list of seventeen people I saw regularly. I thought this would be a difficult exercise, but it was not. The uninspiring people were glaringly so. The lowest number I assigned any one person was a three. Needless to say, I'm not in contact with that person anymore. There was nothing terrible about her, but she was the kind of person who when they speak only complaints come out of their mouth. I was like that too at one time, and I probably would have been a snarky cohort, but now I see it and I want to run!

On the other end, the highest number I assigned was a nine, and that went to three friends. One was my personal trainer Carrie, which made complete sense since she jump-started so much of this for me. Another was one of the ladies in my exercise group who did some incredibly meaningful volunteer work, the kind of work that stopped me in my tracks to ask more. She was inspirational to me. She was the reason I started doing more important volunteer work in the first place, not to mention all the health benefits of volunteering I've mentioned before. I used to joke in class that "when I grow up I want to be her." She lives her beliefs, and there's nothing more inspiring than that. My last nine went to a friend who I feel is truly supportive. I never feel drained around her—in fact, the complete opposite is true. After seeing her I feel *great*! She actually listens to me and understands me. Our conversations are real. She is most definitely part of my tribe. Try this exercise. List the people you spend the most time with and assign each a number based on how inspiring they are to you. If nothing else, you will see where your energy gets lifted up and where it gets drained.

FOLLOW YOUR NORTH STAR

I wanted to take a minute to talk about commitment. Elisha Goldstein wrapped up his mindful living course discussing commitment, so I thought I'd share my thoughts on the subject too. I've written before about how I was a bit adrift in my life. Things happen to me more often than I had planned. I didn't know any better. I cannot overemphasize how having direction and goals and knowing where you are headed changes your life. I am making things happen for myself now. Like Dorothy, I had the power all along, but just didn't realize it. Manifestation is *real*. I see it working in my life every day.

The difference is having intention and commitment to what I want with daily reminders. My reminders come in all forms. Some days, it's in my yoga class. My favorite instructor, who is like my guru, will say just the right thing on the right day. I swear he can read my mind, and my body for that matter. He knows exactly what I need to hear and what I need to do physically! I'm sure I'm not the only one in the class who feels that way, but that's the magic of a brilliant instructor.

Another reminder is good old Post-it notes! These are great to write your intentions on and post them on the dashboard of your car, your bathroom mirror or the refrigerator. Wherever it will be seen! Another way to be reminded of where you are headed is a vision board. I keep mine in my bedroom as a constant reminder. I love it. I've actually used mine for two years straight, as my goals have remained the same, but the week I'm writing this I'm having a vision board party to make a new board with my friends! I used Sarah Centrella's book *#futureboards* as a guide this time, and I'm glad I did. She made me think really big, way bigger than I would have on my own. And this will not be a board for just the coming year. It's my vision for the next ten, twenty or thirty years! I can't wait to put it all together. Have you found your North Star? Do you have reminders in place to keep you committed to your mission? Try one or two of the following:

- Write your intentions on Post-it notes and place them in your car, on your bathroom mirror or on your refrigerator.

- Have a yoga or other meditation practice to keep you mindful and intentional.

- Make a vision board.

PART 8

AWAKENING II

21 Day Meditation Experience Round 3

At this point I was ready to dive into my next 21 Day Meditation Experience with Deepak Chopra. I had gained so much insight into my self I was excited to keep going. This session was called Energize Your Life—Secrets to a Youthful Spirit. When we think of energy we typically think of food fueling us. But Deepak explains there are actually four types of energy: physical (moving), mental (understanding), emotional (caring) and spiritual (meditation).

I am an enthusiastic, high-energy person. That's because I've learned to put things in place in my life that give me energy, not deplete it. I've written many times about finding my tribe and taking toxic people out of my life. After I've met up with girlfriends for lunch or a movie or whatever, my energy is through the roof. I feel like I've had ten cups of coffee, I'm smiling and I feel like I can take on anything. I try to maintain some type of connection with my friends once a week. I'll send a quick text and see if

136

someone wants to meet up. If I see an event I want to go to, I immediately think of which friends in my life would most enjoy it and start contacting them to get it on the calendar!

I have always had this tendency, but since I began this journey and started working on myself I've discovered I'm overflowing with energy. Even though I'm an Upholder, I did not always want or do the right things to maintain the energy I wanted in my life because I just didn't know any better.

According to Deepak, meditation increases and renews our energy. I practice meditation in multiple places in my life, and all of them clear my head in a way that gives me spiritual energy. First is my morning meditation at home, second is my yoga practice and third is my soul writing (more to come on that later!). All three of these practices make it possible for me to move through my day without stress and worry.

On the other hand, a few things do challenge my energy levels. First is cloudy weather. I know that sounds like a small thing, but more now than ever, the weather has a huge impact on how I feel. If I wake up to a warm, sunny day, I feel a surge of energy and happiness. I'm happy just to go to the grocery store! Just to be out in the bright, warm sun feels so good to me! But an overcast day can kill my mood, so the best bet for me to counteract this is to meet up with a friend or exercise in some form, preferably outside. One thing I haven't done yet but want to is to purchase a sun lamp for home. It would be good to have during our cold Northern Virginia winters. How are your energy levels? Start noting what depletes and energizes you. Try the following:

- Meet up with friends who raise your energy level, not deplete it.

- Exercise. Preferably outdoors.

- Meditate regularly.

DAY 2 BUILDING RESILIENCY

I spent the first half of my life with almost zero resiliency. And I paid a high price for that. I had almost no ability to bounce back from setbacks or upsetting situations. According to Deepak, resiliency gives us energy and the ability to rebound mentally and physically with energy. Stress is a *huge* energy drainer. A simple practice of getting enough sleep can help in this area. I have always been an early riser. Always. Just naturally. My mistake was I was still going to bed at 10:00 or 11:00 at night and then getting up at 4:30 or 5:00 in the morning. I didn't feel that bad, but when I made the switch to a 9 or 9:30 bedtime, I felt amazing. I was getting enough sleep and being productive. I'm no longer willing to sacrifice my health and wellness for work, family or anything else. My health is first or everything else goes to crap. I saw it happen in my own house when I was not functional.

Deepak says we must "build a platform by making positive choices *every day.*" Yes, every day is key. This is partly why I think people don't find lasting change with things like Dry January or a Whole 30. Even though I agree wholeheartedly that giving up alcohol and eating an anti-inflammatory diet are important, doing it for a month isn't setting yourself up for meaningful changes in your diet. It has to be a *lifestyle* change. Same for meditation. Doing it once in a while is helpful, but having a regular practice is life changing. These are all the ways we can build our platform as Deepak says.

I maintain these habits by keeping everything in my calendar. I'm a bit of a planner junkie, and I have a couple of systems in place to help with reminders. On my weekly page of my calendar I have a section I call My Morning Routine. In it I have my routine that begins at 5:00 every morning:

- Meditate for fifteen minutes.

- Read fifty pages.

- Do some soul writing.

This is how I start my days. I may meditate or read again later, but starting out this way guarantees it gets done. Another way I use my planner to build my platform is tracking habits. Here I list the five habits I want to maintain every day:

- Hydrate.
- Read.
- Eat meals, not snacks.
- Practice soul writing.
- Meditate.

Some of these overlap with my morning routine. It's another way for me to stay on track. How are you building your platform? Think about where and how you can add habits to your life that would help build your platform of positive choices!

DAY 3 FULFILLMENT!

Do you ever notice how you don't feel tired when life is satisfying? In Day 3's meditation Deepak explained when we have organized energy with meaning and purpose we then have fulfillment in our lives. And we do not accept stress and obstacles. Once again, it's about staying in the flow.

The centering thought for today was: "When I feel fulfilled, I have enough energy for anything needed." This really was a bit of a lightening bolt moment. Ever since I began my journey and started focusing on all the areas of my life (diet, exercise, spirituality, meditation, having goals, being in nature, volunteering, coping skills, conquering fear, becoming an optimist, building community) and basically pursuing *everything* that makes me happy, I have found an energy that just flat out didn't exist before. I'm just *so alive*. I was always a doer. That's not new. My Upholder tendency allows me to get done what I want to get done. The difference was the work I had put in resulted in so much happiness and energy. I can't even relate to people who walk around in the "I'm so tired" state. Think about how many people say that to you in a given day. Or maybe it's you. And I know looking back it wasn't just "one" thing that made this happen for me. It was all the things. I am a work in progress. It is easier to move forward knowing everything I put into this will come back tenfold. I keep moving forward in all areas of my life, and I also keep finding new areas to learn about! Take a minute to think about how fulfilled you are in your life. Does your life give you energy or drain it? Do you have meaning and purpose that fulfill you?

DAYS 4-5 SELF

There is a lot of talk about self-care these days. And for good reason. I think as a society we are starting, very slowly, to realize how important self-care is and that "busyness" should not be a badge of honor.

Usually when we think of self-care we think of exercise, spa treatments, meditation, sleep, etc. Deepak asks us to think about where we put our attention. He explains our creative energy comes from joy. So I ask myself "What brings me joy?" and do more of that. Pretty simple. It's basically the same principle as the Happiness Project. Read more about the Happiness Project here: www.GretchenRubin.com. I knew I was on the right track. This lesson just reinforced what I already knew I had to continue doing.

It feels really good to value myself enough to make my own happiness a priority. As a mom, I put myself second in everything. I lost myself so completely during my kids' younger years that I don't remember doing anything for myself outside of the occasional trips to the salon. I never pursued my hobbies and interests, I didn't read as often as I would have liked, I didn't go out with friends very often, and I didn't volunteer outside of my children's school. My world was small. It was all for them, and that's perfectly fine. I chose that and I wanted it. But looking back, I could have stayed home with them and kept my sense of self by pursing some of these other options. Maybe the buildup of fear and anxiety wouldn't have happened, or at least not to the extreme it did. Who knows? Lesson learned the hard way. Are you finding joy in your everyday life? Are you pursuing your interests and the things that give you the most joy? Try a Happiness Project! It's a *great* way to find and rediscover what you love. I have a series of posts about my Happiness Project on my blog.

DAYS 6-7 AUTHENTICITY

If you are not familiar with Brene Brown, you should be. Her TED Talk, books and now upcoming podcast have been helpful and eye-opening to me, mostly in the realm of authenticity. Deepak says, "Living a life not owned by you is draining. Being yourself is the most fulfilling." Yes, it certainly is. It's obvious. I spent many years, especially in my teens and twenties, not being my authentic self. I was really good at molding myself into whoever I was around. And I continued to do that all the way through my forties. For example, I mentioned before I have bird feeders and I like to bird-watch. I kept this hobby under wraps throughout my adulthood. Why? Because I didn't think anyone else would have an interest and I thought their eyes would glaze over if I told them. But I love it. I love seeing all the different birds at my feeder. I love identifying new birds. I love tracking my Life List to see how many species I've seen, and I love going on birding walks and hikes. So, if I hid this hobby, how was I going to meet someone else who enjoys it? I mean, isn't that the way to make real friendships? Not fake "let's get a drink and do nothing else" friendships. Now when I meet people I'm upfront about all the goofy things I like. I'm so me. And people can take it or leave it. It's amazing how many people I meet who say, "Me too!" when I tell them something I'm really into. So much wasted time not doing that. It's been a long road, but I've learned this now. I'm only halfway through my life, so better to learn it now and make the change than to never have learned it!

Until the reckoning of my mid-forties, I never attempted to be my authentic self. And it makes me sad and a little regretful of my past. But I cannot live there. I can only look forward and be my authentic self from here on out. Some people might drop out of my life and have. And that's okay. When I really am who I am I find the right people to be around. They just show up. I can't explain it! Deepak says we need to do the following to be our most fulfilled:

- Be open and vulnerable.

- Have inner strength.

- Live in the now.

- Increase strengths.

- Be kind.

- Overcome fears.

- Be helpful.

This again was all the things I was working on, more reinforcement I was headed in the right direction. Do you feel like you are being your authentic self? How could you be more true to yourself? I suggest checking out Brene Brown's work at https://brenebrown.com.

DAY 8 INFLAMMATION

The first time someone explained leaky gut to me, I didn't really understand it. I was in the middle of all of my pain with no answers. But my chiropractor was on to something when he explained to me how when we take antibiotics it wipes out not only the bad bacteria but all the good bacteria as well. Not only did my drug reaction cause my injury, it pretty much destroyed my microbiome. Also, when we eat inflammatory foods our small intestine gets inflamed, which then causes particles to leak out of the intestine and into our bloodstream. When this happens our body thinks these are foreign objects it needs to fight. This is the cause of many autoimmune diseases, fibromyalgia and a host of other issues. If you want to know more about leaky gut and the effects on the body, click here: https://www.

health.harvard.edu/blog/leaky-gut-what-is-it-and-what-does-it-mean-for-you-2017092212451. Like I said in the beginning of this book, repairing my leaky gut was huge for me. A forever lifestyle change. Once I knew what inflammatory foods were doing to my body and my brain, it was easy to make the switch.

This week Deepak talked about reducing inflammation for lifelong energy. Yes, an anti-inflammatory diet certainly does give you more energy and so much more. Did you know your gut and brain are connected and that your brain can actually become inflamed? This can cause another whole host of problems related to your nervous system and even to your mood. You can read more about it here: https://www.health.harvard.edu/diseases-and-conditions/the-gut-brain-connection. Did you know meditation reduces inflammation? You can read more here: https://www.huffpost.com/entry/meditation-brain-changes-study_n_56b4b7aee4b04f9b57d-93bef. Meditation brings us peace and calm. Deepak says "Daily stresses won't trigger you as easily."

If you want to reduce inflammation, try an anti-inflammatory diet or a paleo diet. I really don't like the word "diet." It's actually a lifestyle. But you can give it thirty days and see how you feel! I highly recommend *Practical Paleo* by Diane Sanfilippo or *Whole 30* by Melissa Urban.

DAYS 9–10 SITTING TOO MUCH, NOT SLEEPING ENOUGH

Have you heard sitting is the new smoking? Our bodies are designed to move, not sit all day. In fact, we should be moving for five minutes for every hour we are sitting. Moving every hour actually maintains our energy. You can read more about the effects of a sedentary lifestyle here: https://www.huffpost.com/entry/sitting-is-the-new-smokin_b_5890006?guccounter=1&guce_referrer=aHR0cHM6Ly93d3cuZ29vZ2xlLmNvbS8&guce_referrer_sig=AQAAAALZvfyveMZMStcpTuOzWOOVGrZwQCb-FXBDgeCCabrdOM9zuUKjvpLaBZcSVsuIp4UxRWVXJAndpEchMc-

5mKpAdEm8jLRffMpnT-Oq66U6LWj6QXUkZOanURZAUurlE9mn-B1z1NszUS1EK_kYZVL60D9WsKr2UVL2sXkbz8c0fDR.

Over Days 9 and 10 Deepak explained the importance of movement, rest and reducing stress. For a long time I sacrificed sleep. It's still my default go-to shortcut for fitting everything in, but now I'm much more aware and catch myself before I fall into any destructive patterns. I wasn't one to stay up too late, though occasionally I'm guilty of that. For me it was choosing to get up at 4:30 a.m. or 4:45 a.m. on days when I should have slept a little longer to get those seven hours. Typically, I sleep six and a half to seven hours a night. My body rarely needs eight hours of sleep. I have to be sick or sleep deprived for that to happen. Remember, I'm a fairly high-energy person, so lying around in bed doesn't appeal to me. But now I know when we are sleeping our brains are actually getting rid of toxins. Like a big cleanup. This is incredibly important to prevent Alzheimer's, as sleep deprivation can lead to memory problems just for this reason. Read more here: https://www.nih.gov/news-events/news-releases/brain-may-flush-out-toxins-during-sleep.

Sleep was going to become a priority for me. Like most people, I sacrificed sleep for partying or studying in my twenties. I saw zero consequences of this behavior and didn't see it as important at all. In my thirties I sacrificed sleep for my babies and though I did feel that, I still thought that is just part of motherhood. I caught naps here and there, but still did not take care of myself. My forties was the reckoning for all my behavior to this point, along with the injuries that followed. Right now my typical routine is to wake up between 4:30 and 5:00 a.m., depending on which yoga class I'm headed to. I have my morning routine of tea, reading and writing, then out the door I go. On the other days I get up at the same time, have more time for my routine, then head to strengthening class or a hike. My bedtime ideally is 9:30 p.m. This gives me a solid seven hours and life is good. But 10:00 p.m. happens more than I'd like, mostly due to chores around the house, chatting with the family, picking someone up, or being out doing something fun! If I go to bed at 10:00 p.m. for more than a couple of nights in a row, I start getting a cloudy head and meditation becomes more difficult because my body wants to sleep. Do you want to increase your physical energy or hours of sleep? Try the following:

- Set an alarm on your phone to remind yourself to move every hour you have been sitting.

- Set a bedtime alarm along with a wakeup alarm. This is a Gretchen Rubin tip that I love. The bedtime alarm forces you to start that bedtime routine and stick to it!

DAY 11 LIVE BY THIS!

When I was working through this 21 Day Meditation Experience, when someone would say "antiaging" I immediately would think of serums and injections to keep myself looking youthful. But Deepak talks about antiaging as a skill we can master. He calls it the "formula for your life!" Yes, please, tell me more! The seven things people who age well have in common are:

1. Meditation.
2. Wide social circle.
3. Close relationships/friends.
4. Vitamins.
5. Sleep and activity.
6. Curiosity.
7. New challenges.

Some of these areas, like meditation and sleep, I was already working on, and I had activity covered, but I had work to do on the others. First, I needed to widen my social circle. At this time I hadn't jumped into much volunteering yet or started working part-time. But knowing I needed to widen my social circle, along with many other reasons, prompted me to get out and meet more people. My volunteering and new job definitely did that for me. When I was a full-time stay-at-home mom, I had a supportive social circle of other young moms. Period. The end. And there's nothing necessarily wrong with that because I needed those more experienced moms in my life to help me through motherhood. Those relationships were important. But I would have been better off if I would have kept my friendships from work or other areas in my life as well. I had a tendency to let relationships fade if they weren't right in front of me. I don't do that now, but I see that for many, many years this was the norm. When we moved from California to Virginia I hardly kept in touch with my old friends other than Christmas cards and an occasional phone call. Facebook certainly makes this so much easier now.

Having close relationships and friendships is something I'm always working toward. That's not an overnight thing. You need to find your tribe and then make the effort to be a good friend and vice versa. And that second part is out of your control. I'm thankful for the good friends I do have. I don't take them for granted anymore.

Vitamins! This should have been on my New Year's resolution list! I have yet to take any supplements, and that is mostly because what I've read about them has me confused. I'm not a fan of the fact that they aren't regulated in any way. And because of that, when they are tested things show up that are not listed in the ingredients and other things that are listed aren't in them at all. I find so much fraud a bit dangerous. On the other hand, if I knew they were clean, there are some I would take. This is an upcoming to-do for me!

Curiosity falls under my Happiness Project theme of "Saying Yes." I consider saying yes part of continuous learning and trying new things. I've tried more new things in the past two or three years than I could count. I never in a million years thought I'd be a class exercise type person, a yogi, a hiker, a blogger, an activist, a writer, a library aide or a notary public. If

I wouldn't have tried those things, my life wouldn't be nearly as happy or rich as it is today.

New challenges is similar to curiosity. but I look at this through the lens of fear. Without fear I can challenge myself to actually write this book. Without fear I can go for those yoga poses I never would have considered before. Without fear I can walk long distances without pain. Without fear I can learn how to nature sketch. Without fear I can go back to work and learn a new skill set and meet new people. Without fear I can set a real budget and work on it every single day. All of these things were challenges for me, but if it doesn't make you a little nervous, then it's not a big enough challenge!

The key is to continue working on all seven of these areas for the rest of your life. That is antiaging. At the time, I wrote in my notebook: "Live by this!!" That makes me smile today. How many of the seven areas do you feel you are working on in your life? Do you see areas where you could improve? Use this list as a guide. Place Post-its in your bathroom or in your car. Or make a vision board using these areas as a guide for how you want to live.

DAYS 12-15 MINDSET SHIFT

As I came to the end of my 21 Day Meditation Experience, the focus became more on who we are and our own journey. Deepak says, "You are what you think." This is true on so many levels. He explains we are a projection of our core beliefs and those beliefs become actions and truths we live by. When you have an aha moment a shift occurs and your beliefs change. This is basically the truth of my entire journey and why I finally felt the need to get it out to the world! I had a couple of major aha moments. First was my realization that my pain was not all physical. Second, I learned how important having true purpose was. Third, overcoming fears is the key to moving forward in life. And fourth, authenticity is freedom. These are the broad strokes of what I learned. And this book is basically breaking all that down for you. But each of these was a mindset reset and a major aha moment that took me in a new and different direction. The bottom line is that what I was doing wasn't working for me anymore. I needed a new way to live. It became my focus to "get better at life" rather than to continue living in pain and fear.

Deepak says we need to go beyond our story. We get stuck there. I'm not good at this or that, I can't … (fill in the blank). We give ourselves these labels and then we tend to live by them. I certainly did that. Fear dominated everything I did. Now, I just do. There is so much happiness and freedom in that. When you open yourself up to living, life becomes amazing. Have you had an aha moment that created a mind shift for you?

DAY 16 RESCUE ME!

Day 16 hit me right over the head immediately with this statement. "No one will rescue you." For a long time, I counted on others to do things for me in every way. Whether it was my parents, my spouse, a friend or a coworker. I lived my life in a way that allowed me to feel secure that someone else would pick up the pieces of my mistakes and carelessness. This could be my financial situation, a speeding ticket, something broken in the house or my car needing repairs. I never until very recently took ownership of these things myself. I would go to someone else for help. Every. Time. Not that we shouldn't have supportive people in our lives when it's truly needed, but that's not what I was doing. I knew and chose to behave in such a way that I eventually would need rescuing. At some point in this journey of mine I got very tired of relying on others. I started fixing (what I could) myself so as to not wait for what I wanted. It may not be "right," but it was done. And done by me. Our finances was another area of fantastical thinking that somehow I could magically pay for college, get out of debt and still retire well. Maybe someone would rescue me from this disaster. I realized no one was going to take control of our finances if I didn't. So I did. I read every book I could find on personal finance and listened to every podcast and started putting all the advice I was hearing into action. On my own. No rescuing. I'm really proud of how much I've learned. We are now debt free (not including the mortgage, but that is next) and have emergency savings and a budget I work on daily.

For most of my life I felt I could get away with a lot because of the way I was treated, mostly by men. People seemed to want to rescue me and I let it happen, mostly in the '80s and '90s, but if I wanted to play that up today, I could. But I would not ever want to be that person again because so much weakness is there. I love being strong and more independent. It's a great feeling! Along with being physically stronger, it makes for a powerful combination. I feel unstoppable. I fell back on the "poor me, rescue me" attitude for way too long.

Deepak says we prefer denial to actually looking at our situation. And what we are aware of we can change. Awareness is everything. Deepak explains, "Whatever you are not aware of you cannot change." This is where change happens. Once you are aware of your reality, you can change it. I think this is what happened to me. I suddenly was listening to a variety of podcasts, listening to these women and all they were accomplishing and I thought *I could do that! I want to do what they are doing!* And so change began. Awareness = Change. Are there areas of your life where you feel like you are avoiding change? Or are you in denial about your reality? Take time to meditate on this to become closer to your true self. Change comes with awareness.

DAYS 19-21 FINAL THOUGHTS

These meditation practices are so healing for me. It's what I imagine therapy must be like. I probably should have had some therapy along the way. Deepak ended by talking about wholeness being a completely healed state. Deepak explains that "we can meditate our problems to solutions and that allows us to be a healing force."

Knowing I have the power to heal myself and others is pretty amazing. It truly is an awakening (hence the name of my blog). I am now awake. I was not before. These are true statements. And it's pretty obvious when walking through this world how many people are not awake. I'm thankful every day I'm no longer living that way. I'm not only a happier person, but everyone around me is happier (emotional contagion) as well. I can speak my mind forcefully but respectably. These may sound like lessons for a child, but somewhere along the line these areas were missed in my youth. Better late than never.

PART 9

HAPPINESS AND GOAL SETTING

Be Happier

One of the many books I read during this time in my life was *The 10 Keys to Happier Living* by Vanessa King. I love this book. It's extremely straightforward and gave me lots of little tips and tools I put into practice right away. King explains that the following list is "based on an extensive review of the latest research about what really helps people flourish. These are not 'ten commandments,' because each of us is unique and what works for one of us may not for someone else. They are simply ten areas that tend to make a big difference to our happiness—and are within our control." Called "The GREAT DREAM," it is as follows:

GIVING	Do for others.
RELATING	Connect with people.
EXERCISING	Take care of your body.
AWARENESS	Live life mindfully.
TRYING OUT	Keep learning new things.
DIRECTION	Have goals to look forward to.
RESILIENCE	Find ways to bounce back.
EMOTIONS	Look for what's good (gratitude).

| ACCEPTANCE | Be comfortable with who you are. |
| MEANING | Be part of something bigger. |

Do you see a lot of familiar themes here? I certainly did. I decided from now on, when I make my New Year's resolutions and goals, I will make sure I hit each of these areas. I wrote in my notebook "Use this for 2019 goals." And I did. It's very easy for me to let one or two slip, maybe the ones that are the hardest. For me that would be acceptance, resilience and giving.

Acceptance of what is and acceptance of others for who they are and not trying to "fix" them is a constant struggle for me. I think it is partially my Enneagram 1 Reformer (more on that to come) personality playing out. But I did learn from Deepak Chopra that everyone is where they are supposed to be on their journey. I cannot change that. I can be an example and that's about it. Unless someone asks specifically for help, I need to accept who they are at this moment.

I'm also very self-critical. I've learned from my study of the Enneagram, and me being a 1 means not only do I want to change others and change the world to do what is "right" I also have a running self-critic in my head that tells me all the things I've done wrong.

Resilience is a learning process for me. If you've read my blog from the beginning, you know I had almost zero coping skills and focused on having them right from the start of my recovery. I have found the most helpful ways for me to bounce back are meditation, music, reading, support from friends and problem-solving.

Saying I need to work on giving doesn't make me sound like the best person, but I don't have the best track record in this department. I do give. However, I really need to step outside myself and my world more and help those around me. I am good at helping on a big picture level. That's the activist in me. I get so worked up and feel the need to do and give, but sometimes I lose sight of those right in front of me who need help. It's a work in progress. Have you thought about ways you could be happier? Take a look at the list above and come up with some goals to fill in the gaps of where you could improve.

GOAL SETTING

There's a lot of information out there about goal setting. I never paid any attention to goal setting until recently. I wasn't someone who set any goals for myself. Ever. I like challenges, and by nature I'm a doer and I'm organized, but true, structured short- and long-term goals? Never happened. Until now! Having goals propels us into growth. Without them life just happens to us. We are adrift.

In *The 10 Keys to Happier Living* the author suggests crafting goals with five "how-tos."

1. Be Specific: Identify the what, where, when, how, how much or how many.

2. Know Your Why: Have a clear reason.

3. "Will Do" not "Won't Do": Frame goals as what I will do, not what I won't do.

4. Growth Goals (Not Being Seen as Good): Goals should about doing better, not being the best.

5. Write Down and Share: Write your goals down and share your progress.

I was currently using two of these how-tos correctly, numbers two and four. I for sure knew my why. It's the entire reason I started this wellness journey in the first place! To be pain free! For number four, I never had interest in being "the best" at something when setting my goals. Even now I don't strive for that. I have goals for my yoga practice, but I'm not there to be the best in my class. I just want to progress in my poses and increase my mindfulness while doing so.

I did change my goals to include more specifics. For example, instead of "read more" my reading goal for this year is to read one hundred books. I then broke that down to reading a minimum of fifty pages a day, in the morning. This hit the "what, when and how much." It definitely keeps me on track.

Three was interesting because I did have a goal of eating meals, not snacks. And that's exactly how I worded it. A better goal would be "Eat three complete, healthy meals every day," because when I do that I don't snack or if I do it's minimal. Good tip!

I was writing down my goals but not sharing them until I discovered Gretchen Rubin's podcast and began her eighteen for 2018, nineteen for 2019 "goals" list. Then I began sharing everything in the Happier in Hollywood Facebook group (Gretchen's sister's podcast). It's great getting the feedback and I have a ton of accountability partners. Also, when we share our goals they become real. I remember the first time I told anyone I was writing a book. The only person who knew was me! But here I was meeting someone for the first time, and it just popped out of my mouth. I figured if I just start saying it, it will propel me forward to complete it. I became a writer at that moment. A writer writing their first book. Since then I've told a ton of people. You never know where a conversation will lead or what the universe has in store for you! Are you someone who sets goals? How do you go about setting them? Try the steps above to help you get clarity on what you want your goals to be.

GOAL SETTING PART 2

After learning how to craft my goals I created my Big Goal as suggested in *The 10 Keys to Happier Living*. My Big Goal was "To Have a Job with Purpose," with three scenarios.

Scenario number 1   Become a Health Coach
Scenario number 2   Become a Food Advocate/Politics
Scenario number 3   Write a Book

Next was my Common Sub Goal, which was "Finish Health Coaching Certification."

My Specific Sub Goals looked like this.

- Read/use Christy Whitman's business book.

- Look into part-time work in this field.

- Listen to wellness podcasts.

- Look into food advocacy.

- Have a website.

- Start a blog.

- Start writing a book.

It's amazing to me to see where all of this started. Looking at my three scenarios, I have achieved the goal of becoming a health coach. And I'm in the process of writing my book as I type this! I'm still working on the food advocacy/politics goal, but it is in the works! I also achieved some of my Sub Goals. I had started my blog! I also started writing my book, and I'm currently researching ways I want to get involved in food advocacy and public health. I actually have read Christy Whitman's book *Business Boutique* and I loved it. I'm just not ready at this time to use what I've learned. Currently I'm working part-time, not in the wellness industry, but in another love of mine, the library. After I've written my book I plan to launch a health coaching business and set up my website, and at that time I'll dive into using Christy's book.

I'm happy with how things are going right now. I'm working in a field I love. I'm also blogging and writing within the health and wellness space I want to be in in the future. Win-win!

GOAL SETTING PART 3

At this point I was discovering so many teachers and really finding a new way of life. One podcast led to a book, that led to a program, that led to a class, that led to new friends. Life was rolling along, and I was learning everything I could along the way, seeing improvements in myself, my life and everything around me.

During this time I heard Mel Robbins speak on one of many podcasts I listen to. I started following her, and in January 2019 I completed her Mindset Reset program. Mel doesn't beat around the bush. She's up-front and honest. Her program and approach woke me up and got me moving on a lot of things that were just ideas in my head. For Mel, it's all about taking action. And I had learned just what taking action could do for me; now I was going to take it to another level.

Getting back to goals, Mel says you must do a visualization exercise for every goal you have. If you haven't done visualization before, you basically imagine yourself doing the very thing you are aiming to achieve. Not only are you picturing it, but you need to feel the positive emotions that come with the visualization because your brain doesn't know the difference between real memories and visualization. She suggests doing this practice for thirty seconds every day. This way you are developing the skill as if you were actually doing it. That's amazing! https://www.huffpost.com/entry/visualization-goals_b_878424

My morning routine includes my meditation time and reading, among other things, so I decided to add visualization time. What I love about this process is the overall impact it has when I'm dedicating only a small amount of my time to the practice. Have you done a visualization exercise to help achieve your goals? Close your eyes and see yourself doing that thing you want to achieve. Give it try!

PART 10 AWAKENING III

LIFE CHANGING GRATITUDE

I'm going to dive back into Deepak's 21 Day Meditation Experience. This time the subject was manifesting grace through gratitude. Deepak explains that gratitude makes a connection to grace. It is actually a physical change.

It's hard to be unhappy when you are focused on gratitude. Instead of spending time wanting more and more (more clothes, more furniture, better cars, more trips), learn how to be truly grateful for what you have. After going through the horror of my pain experiences, I was and still am so grateful for all the small things. Because when all the small things are taken from you they become the big things. As I was doing more, the more grateful I became for being able to drive again, to use my computer and to have the ability to read for ten minutes a day. I was incredibly grateful when I could start taking pain-free walks and being out in nature—the list goes on and on. These are things I didn't think twice about before the pain. Even when I was still not fully functional I would do my nightly gratitude practice. It's not easy when you feel awful, but here is an example of a couple of my gratitude notebook entries in 2018.

January 27

A compliment from an old friend

Sitting in the sun reading

Finished a wonderful book

A nice dinner out

A really good night's sleep

February 13

Good visit with Dr. B

Fun exercise classes. Everyone was happy today.

Tippy is feeling better.

Enjoying the Olympics

A laugh with a stranger on an elevator

These are not big things. But I was grateful for each and every one of them. So grateful. Next, I listed the people in my life who I'm grateful for. (I used initials here in place of names.)

M for loving me.

M for her point of view and support.

M for always being there for me.

N for being real.

D for his guidance.

My physical therapists for helping me feel better.

N for his heart.

O for her kindness.

C for seeing my strength when I couldn't.

A for being an example of what I want to be.

S for understanding me.

There are personal stories behind each and every one of these people, but the point is when I list them I can see how each one has had a huge impact in my life and I'm certainly grateful for them all. Do you have a gratitude practice? All it takes is a dollar store notebook and pen! Start today!

DAY 2 ELEVATE YOURSELF

Taking the gratitude notebook practice to the next level was what I got out of the next day's practice. Not only was I to list three to five things I am grateful for, but then to say thank you for them. This is where grace happens. We are changing pathways in our brains, according to Deepak Chopra. This daily practice will elevate your gratitude practice into something you can feel and experience.

The day of this particular meditation I wrote the following:

Today's three good things:

- My family.

- A nourishing meal.

- Birds at the feeder.

Simple gratitude. Taking the time to recognize these things was the change for me. Visualize the thankfulness.

Next I was to recall a time when I told someone how much I appreciated them. That was easy—it was when I told my personal trainer Carrie how much I appreciate her. I try to tell her as often as I can. When I told her, instead of a blanket "thank you," she told me how much she appreciated that I trust her. I didn't expect that! See what happens when you start sharing your gratitude? It comes right back at you!

A few takeaways for me from these exercises was to not just robotically write down five things I'm grateful for each night. I needed to express my gratitude to those I was maybe taking for granted or someone who should know how much I appreciate them. I decided to do the following:

- Be more considerate of what my husband, Mike, wants.

- Write a note or give a small gift to A.

- Don't be bitchy around Carrie because of the changes she made to her program.

Yes, I got very upset when I heard Carrie was making changes to the program I loved so much! I saw it as the end of my progress, but it was just the beginning. Carrie was just trying to move forward in her business and I took it extremely personally. Mistake! The truth is, the changes led me down another path where I increased my yoga (which I desperately needed to do) and allowed me to try different strength classes at my local rec center. Now I'm taking classes I never would have considered myself ready for, and guess what? I'm just fine! And getting stronger all the time! I was ready but needed a big push. A really big push. Why is it I don't do what I'm supposed to do until things are completely taken away from me or are completely upended? But here it was happening. This was the universe at work again. Every time I think I've hit a wall or something has happened that I find devastating and I become hysterical crying, I find it results in bigger and better things in my life. Every single time. Sometimes we can't see how the universe is working, but it always is. Try a gratitude practice that includes a thank you visualization. Let yourself feel the emotions that come with that practice.

DAY 3 IT'S THE LITTLE THINGS

"It's the little things" is something I always say because it truly is. Gratitude can come from the most simple things. It's the multitude of these little things adding up to the whole that creates happiness. This week I was to list a few simple things that made me happy. Here we go:

- Seeing the birds at my feeders.
- Flowers.
- Walks in the warm sunshine.
- Hot baths.

When I have a day that hits all of these things, I'm generally very happy. They are mood boosters in the most simple way. I'm grateful for them.

Then I was to think of a recent experience I enjoyed. For me it was a recent concert my husband and I attended. We are both music lovers and see a lot of shows. One of my favorites was seeing U2 a few years ago. I've been a fan for thirty-two years! But this was my first time seeing them. I absolutely love being in the presence of the artists I love and appreciate so much. And sharing that with thousands of other people is such a communal experience. Few things make me as happy as going to a show. It can be transcending.

I am a big morning person. No surprise there, but during this time in my life I became utterly obsessed with sunrises. The absolute stunning beauty of the sunrise floored me. And sunrises are so peaceful. I love the combination of the early morning, the quiet and the beauty. This is something to be grateful for! Think about the small things you are grateful for. Make a list and then continue to use a gratitude notebook to record simple pleasures. Before you know it you will have an entire year's worth of things to look back on and see the richness of your life.

DAY 4 BUILDING MY TRIBE!

At this point in my journey I found myself involved in several new adventures. I was attending my new yoga studio regularly and had gotten to know the teachers and other students. It was another new group. I was also getting involved in local politics, becoming an activist without even realizing it. I began to see friends on a regular basis: lunches, movies, book signings, coffee, you name it.

My tribe was building and it felt amazing. Suddenly I had the group I had wanted and needed in my life. It's all about making the effort and taking action when it came to all the changes I was making in my life, and this was no different. Every area of my wellness wheel had action steps.

Nothing happens if you just look at a Post-it with a slogan on it every day. That will not change your life. It's about knowing what you need to do and then taking steps, even tiny ones, every single day toward your end goals. Suddenly life just gets better.

Deepak says this is grace working in our lives. According to Deepak, when we express gratitude, grace responds. Suddenly you are in the flow and moving forward in your life. Things become effortless, he says. It's a shift I felt and still feel 100 percent.

DAY 5 CONSUMERISM

Let's talk about consumerism for a minute. I'm a product of the '70s and '80s. My teen years were spent in the '80s during the height of consumerism. We wanted everything and the best of everything at that. Everything was big and more. How many earrings can you fit on one ear? As many as possible. This way of thinking never really left me. In the '90s I was building my life. I got married, had children, bought a home, bought another larger home, and then bought yet another larger home. We had luxury cars and our kids never went without. I shopped for sport, buying new wardrobes for myself and the kids every season. We went on multiple expensive vacations a year. I remember one in particular when we went to Disney World for more than a week, Hilton Head a week and another week in New York. Excessive to say the least. And this spending continued for years and years until one day it was time to send our oldest to college.

At the same time I was getting our finances in order I was reading about minimalism and basically our throwaway society. I was also becoming much more aware of the environment, plastic pollution and climate change. All of this together suddenly made me rethink how I was living. The meditation work I was doing was also leading me down this path of where true happiness lies. And let me tell you it's not in the stuff. I no longer shop for sport. I shop when I actually need something, not when I want it. I'll need to replace a few things seasonally and I will. But I no longer spend recklessly. And I never, ever pay full price for anything. It's not necessary with all the cool apps to help you with codes and cash back! If you want to read more about rejecting consumerism, you can find more information here:

https://simple.money/issue-03/excess-consumerism/.

The best way to describe it is as a mindset shift that happened over time. Deepak says, "Nothing is enough when not in the present moment. We are never satisfied. When we express thanks, we are aligned with the universe." I also suggest reading Cait Flanders's book *A Year of Less*. I loved this book, and it really made me look at my own life, get out of debt and reject consumerism.

DAY 6 FACING OBSTACLES

Facing obstacles was not something I handled well for most of my life. Avoid, avoid, avoid: that was my answer, especially with money. I kept pushing the problems further down the road and prayed they would figure themselves out. In my new way of looking at life I viewed my money worries as a chance to change. I could see our spending habits and I could now see ways to make improvements. Which we did! We are living debt free. Total freedom! I'm so on top of our financial situation, it's actually fun.

Another area where I constantly would and still do hit obstacles is my neck and back issues. I see these obstacles as reminders to exercise the correct way. This is really about discipline for me. As an Upholder, I tend to "tighten," which means I make rules beyond the rules. I can and have taken things to the extreme. My current battle with this is with my yoga practice. I love yoga so, so much. The upholder in me wants to practice every single day, perfect the poses I can do and learn to do the more difficult poses, attend every workshop and go off on yoga retreats with my studio. And if I actually did all those things, my neck and back would flare up pretty badly. Yoga is fantastic for my spine issues; however, too much of a good thing is not a good thing. I have to balance it. On my calendar

I have two days carved out for strengthening of some kind—kettlebells or other strength training. I have four days dedicated to yoga and one day for a hike or indoor track walk. It's always an internal battle on those strength days. My heart is saying, "Go to yoga again!" But I have to remember it's the strengthening that helped me get out of pain and keeps me going. Yoga has helped with the pain too, but in a different way. And 100 percent of the time, when I'm in my strengthening class I feel great and realize I should probably be doing it more.

The third area where I hit obstacles is with my kids. Don't we all! The bottom line is my kids are learning to be adults now. They are seventeen and twenty. I can't save them from everything. The lessons learned at this age are big ones. Big kids, big issues. I've learned to be in the flow. I don't work myself up about them like I used to. I'm not saying I don't worry about them. I do. But it's more guiding them through than sitting back and worrying.

Deepak says we should open ourselves up to obstacles. "There is a gift in every moment. Obstacles are not your enemy. Take a fresh look at the situation." That is what I did with every one of the issues I discussed earlier. Take a look at any obstacles in your own life. How could you reframe them to see the grace and gifts they provide you?

DAYS 7-9 STORIES

As much progress as I'd made to this point, I would occasionally wonder what could have been if I hadn't had all these health issues. This is not a good road to venture down. For so long I was focused only on the negative. I was consumed with pain. It was a constant battle to focus on the positive and move forward, but I did it. I realized too I should have been much more in charge of my own health. I don't necessarily follow all of what a doctor tells me. I use my common sense as well as listen to what I'm told. The difference is when I was younger I would follow the doctor's instructions to a tee, even if inside it didn't feel right, and never questioning.

It's hard for some people to understand what a gift I was given with these events in my life. You hear people say that after a tragedy occurs and you think that can't possibly be how they feel. But it is. Every single part of my life is better because of what happened to me. Just to name a few, I fixed my diet, I did another Happiness Project, I learned how to meditate, I learned how to exercise with correct form, I learned yoga and I made a ton of new friends. Each of those areas ricocheted into many more areas of improvement. A big self improvement, self-healing journey.

Deepak says no two people see reality the same way. Reality is personal (the stories you tell yourself). This was a big aha moment for me. The fact that there even could be stories I was telling myself was a new idea. What do you mean? You mean every thought in my head isn't based on facts? I catch myself in this one all the time. Am I making up a story in my head? Or is this based in facts I know are true. This is life changing when you are aware of it. Deepak says that "we are the author of our life story." I love that so much. I'm just going to keep living my truth. I hope you will too. Do you feel like you are telling yourself a story about what is happening in your life? Or is it based on actual facts? It's a good question to ask yourself. Often. Once you start asking, you can see where you can let go of a lot of anxiety and worry.

DAYS 10-12 YOU ARE WORTHY

"When you believe you are worthy you will attract abundance into your life and success starts to line up for you." These were the words that caught my attention on Day 12 of my Meditation Experience. Deepak says, "Life should be a rising arch of abundance."

I had a lot to think about here. My journal notes from this day are hard for me to read, but it is my truth at the time so here we go. I wrote: "I wasn't brave. I was afraid of everything and everyone. I had no purpose other than motherhood. And even that I could have done better. Never as kind as I could have been."

It makes me so sad to read these words. But this is how I felt and the realization I made. Things are so different now. I've overcome most of my fear because now I know everything I want in life is on the other side of it. And I know feeling the fear is normal. You just have to move forward. "Feel the fear and do it anyway" is basically my life mantra. I was afraid to start yoga, I was afraid to take a leadership role with my current volunteer group, I was afraid to start this blog, I was afraid to write a book, I was afraid to look for a job, I was afraid to go back to school and it just goes on and on. The reason I could do all these things is because I didn't let the fear define me. I moved ahead despite the fear.

I was so wrapped up in myself I rarely reached out to others in need. I make a point to reassess myself constantly. Have I checked in on that friend who is going through a hard time? Am I giving back? Am I making the changes in the world I want to see? Am I kind to everyone? I ask myself these questions often. I always will work on this during meditation. There are guided meditations for everything! Do you feel worthy of abundance? Do you see the law of attraction working in your life? Once you start asking these questions, you may see things in a new light!

DAYS 13-15 ARE YOU JUDGY?

I'll admit I have a tendency to judge others. In this political climate I have found some friends and acquaintances and I don't see eye to eye on a lot of issues. And now with all of us posting our stances and feelings on social media (and I don't have a problem with that because I do it on a regular basis). I am confronted with differing opinions from my own daily. Deepak says, "When you judge another human, you are denying that we are the same." He explains a practice of visualizing the person you are judging with a parental attitude. We need to loosen the grip on our grudges and find compassion. He goes on to say that empathy links you to everyone on earth. That was just mind-blowing to me. Of course it does! My favorite quote of Deepak's from this session was "Step down from the judge's chair."

Yes, Mona step down. And stay down and post this all over your house so you remember!

Next I made a list of people I have judged or continue to judge and found things we both value or something I value and respect about them. Without listing names, I came up with the following:

> Friend/Acquaintance #1: She is extremely giving with her time and her kids.
>
> Friend/Acquaintance #2: She is a good mother.
>
> Friend/Acquaintance #3: We both want the best for our kids. We both are book lovers.

When you start looking at others this way it's much easier to "step down from the judges chair" and stop the internal battle of "I'm right," which I do struggle with. I've found this little exercise can help me get through and not cut these people out of my life just because I disagree with something they did/said or believe. This is not the same as me removing toxic people from my life! That is different and necessary! Have you found yourself judging others? Take some time to try the visualization I described.

DAYS 16-21 WHAT I LEARNED

Wrapping up my 21-Day Meditation Experience I realized how much I had learned and grown in my practice. Being grateful was so much more than writing down five things every night. That part of my practice is solid and the base of everything else, but what I've learned is to "sit in those feelings" when they are happening. Take the time to really feel the joy and gratitude when things are going well. If you don't feel it and you are just writing things down, it won't have the same effect on your brain. And I do have memories from the past that are so good and so vivid that I can still feel them. Events big and small. Big events like when my children were born or that feeling of falling in love when my husband and I were dating. But small things too. I vividly remember a day in my early twenties. At this time I was living close to the beach, and occasionally I would ride my bike from my apartment to the beach and bike along the strand to the next beach town and back to my apartment. This day in particular is a great memory for me, and I can't explain why other than I remember feeling extremely independent and free. I can still remember how the sun felt so warm that day and I also remembering feeling strong. I was working out regularly, but biking was new for me. I loved it.

This experience also made me glaringly aware of how much I judge. Awareness is key. This is something I'm now working on more than ever. I'm an Enneagram 1, the Reformer—by nature I like to "fix things." That includes myself and others. The Enneagram is not exactly a personality test; it's more your true nature. I'm all about self-knowledge! If you want to know more about the Enneagram, you can read more here::https://www.enneagraminstitute.com/type-descriptions.

PART 11

---

21 DAY MEDITATION
EXPERIENCE ROUND 4

I began my fourth Meditation Experience in July 2019. This was my fourth go around, and I was excited to get started. This time the focus was on relationships. Deepak says, "We are not our feelings. Our true selves are always fully awake." Being authentic has been a focus for me ever since I started learning from Brene Brown, Deepak Chopra and Gretchen Rubin. How much time did I spend not being authentic, surrounding myself with those whom I truly had no connection and not really enjoying the things I loved and made me happy?

There was a time when I would meet someone new and I would hear myself edit my conversation as I was speaking. Maybe I did not tell the entirety of my story. And for what? What does not being authentic do for me? I'm meeting someone new, I'm looking for that bond or I'm thinking this could be a new friendship, so don't scare them away! If I fall in that trap, I stop and correct it, being my true self instead.

DAYS 3-4 MIND, BODY, SPIRIT

We have all seen the positive slogans. They abound everywhere. You have these slogans on your phone, on your water bottle, on your clothes, just about anywhere. But, unless you have done the work behind the slogan, what does it really mean? Not a heck of a lot. If you stare at a Post-it note on your mirror that says, "Be Grateful," are you really going to be more grateful? I think not. But if you have a daily gratitude practice and then you see your Post-it on the mirror, the reminder has much more significance. You can feel it, not just read it.

Deepak says if we take care of our mind, body and spirit every day, our relationships will blossom. I find that to be so true. This was a reminder to me to pay attention to the intentions I set for myself and reevaluate. I set the following goals for myself:

- Extend my meditation practice to fifteen minutes a day.

- Stay hydrated—track again.

- Monitor sleep habits—get seven hours a night.

At this point I was meditating regularly in the morning for about five to ten minutes. I had done a few longer sessions, but now I wanted to progress with my practice. This took a little longer to get comfortable with. I bounced around with different guided meditations and I tried just music until I found a few meditations I really enjoy. Now my practice flows between ten and fifteen minutes, depending on the day.

Staying hydrated was a goal I was tracking in my planner. Somewhere along the line I stopped, so in this case it was obvious to me I needed to track it in order to accomplish it. I still do this daily. Between my morning hot green tea, cold green tea after my workout and water in the afternoon, I get it all in.

I've never been one to have much trouble getting to or staying asleep. Only when I was in pain did I have trouble. But because I'm an early riser

I need to stay on track with my bedtime. If I stay up past 10:00 p.m., I feel it the next day. I have a daily alarm set for 4:45 a.m., which gives me just under seven hours of sleep. I know my body doesn't need more than that because I couldn't sleep much longer even if I wanted to. My body likes to be up doing in the morning! Before I started monitoring my sleep I was in the seven hour range, but I noticed I had too many nights where I was at five hours. I can function, but not well. I become irritable and I make mistakes. Having a clear bedtime made this all much easier.

DAYS 5-6 LIKE A ROADMAP TO MY LIFE

"Fear of accepting that I'm just not as 'book smart' as some others." This was what I wrote about myself on Day 5. Not having a degree would sometimes make me feel like an outcast in social situations where I live, as we have the most degreed population in the country. It gets very uncomfortable, depending on the crowd I'm around at the moment. Deepak says, "True self esteem means to rest in the self." Our self-image is built over the years, and to the ego our self-image is everything.

Next I was to list positive attributes about myself. Don't judge! These are just the feelings I had based on my life experiences.

- Motivated.

- Organized.

- Honest.

- Caring.

- Green eyes.

- Pretty/nice figure.

- Reader.

- Varied interests.

- Take good care of myself.

- Good mother.

- Responsible.

- Empathetic.

Making a list like that was not something I'd ever done before. It does make you quite uncomfortable to start. What great things can I say about myself? Not something I do! But why not? Just looking at the list I feel proud of who I am. Okay, so I don't have my degree. But that does not mean I'm not intelligent. Life circumstances stopped me in my tracks while I was in college and I never finished. Life changed and a few years ago I did earn my holistic health certification, and I'm really proud of that. When I finished my certification I was overwhelmed with ideas of what I wanted to do. I wanted and still want to do it all. Should I pursue a job working for a doctor or wellness center? Should I do one-on-one coaching? Should I do group coaching? Should I conduct seminars or online coaching? The list goes on and on. Then during this meditation series I had an aha moment when I realized what I wanted to do first was write a book and tell my story. I wrote in my notebook: "I feel the need to get it all out there to help others. I dream of being an author and someone who can help others with my story. I have no experience in writing, but I'm doing it anyway. I just have this pull to do it and get all the words out. There is a story there. Write a book and share it on my blog."

Well, there it is. I had my answer of what I was going to do! These meditation experiences have been revolutionary and truly life changing. It's made me think through every problem or opportunity in my life. Working through the journaling at the end of each session really got to the core of my being. The words would flow out like a roadmap to my life. I really believe that.

DAYS 7-8 HANG ON!

As I moved through my Meditation Experience, thinking about relationships in my life, both with family and friends, a few things became clear. My son was growing up. At this time he was nineteen years old and in his first year of college. I've come to grips with the fact that he has other things he wants to do now than hang out with his mom! But I miss hanging out with him terribly. This is not a unique situation. Everyone with grown children would probably tell a similar story. But that doesn't make it any less painful. I was losing him. I felt like (and still do) that things are happening in fast-forward and I'm just trying to hang on as he moves forward. I can barely catch up with my feelings as he moves on to the next new thing. I wasn't used to the idea of him living in a dorm when suddenly we were getting him his apartment for the following year. And at the same time he was asking us to send him abroad to study. I hadn't even adjusted to him not living at home fully and suddenly all this was happening. It felt fast. Really fast. That's all I can say. I never feel ready. Things just keep moving forward. I think when our kids are little and things move forward, we parents are in control. We can manage it easier. But when they are adults that control is gone.

When I'm feeling out of control I try to reframe the situation and tell myself he is growing into a strong adult. At some point he's got to be off and running on his own. When I was his age I had my own apartment (with a roommate) with no one supporting me. I worked a full-time corporate job and went to school at night. I found my own doctors, made my own appointments and began saving for a condo. When I think about it that way, he really doesn't need me as much as I think he does.

Deepak says, "Love is essential as a human." Love changes with the different seasons of our lives. I will always miss that little boy who wanted to be with me every hour of every day. When I see other moms and little boys I tend to tear up, I miss him so much. It is painful. The love we have for our children can be overwhelming! I can't wait to see all the wonderful things he does with his life and I will continue to "hang on" as he builds a life of his own.

DAYS 9-10 YOU CAN'T ATTRACT WHAT YOU DON'T HAVE

What I learned about the law of attraction is that "you can't attract what you don't have," as Oprah would say. It took me a while to figure this one out. If you look at this through the eyes of relationships, as I was at this time in my Meditation Experience, what I want out of my relationships is support, listening, being open to new ideas and different ways of thinking, kindness, deep conversations and someone to share all my favorite things.

Deepak says, "You attract what you are." There's so much there. What are you? How do you behave? If I wanted people in my life who behaved as I stated above, then I would need to behave that way too so I could attract it into my life. Deepak also says, "We radiate what we want to bring into our lives and what we seek out is seeking you." I've addressed the law of attraction in previous chapters, but here I'm specifically talking about relationships. If I don't show the people in my life the kind of love and support I want, why should I expect it back? This is a great reminder when I get irritated with someone in my family for not supporting me or not listening. But when I turn that back on myself, I can ask, have I been supportive to them? Have I been listening?

Once we understand this, we can see the law of attraction working in our lives. If you want to know more about the Law of Attraction, you can read more here: https://www.huffpost.com/entry/the-law-of-attraction-exp_b_8430270. Think about what you want to attract into the relationships in your life and ask yourself if you are what you want to attract. What could you do differently to attract what you want in your relationships?

DAYS 11-12 WHAT IS THE QUALITY OF YOUR ENERGY?

Remember what I said about emotional contagion. In some ways, the energy you bring into a room takes on the same contagiousness. Deepak says, "When you walk into a room, you bring your energy with you. Everyone can feel it. We choose what we send into the world." Deepak explains the difference between a Dynamic Life and an Active Life. A lot of us have Active Lives (mental activities and rushing around and ending up feeling empty). In a Dynamic Life your energy has a purpose.

This got me thinking of my own life before and after my injury. I most definitely had the Active Life prior to my injury—rushing, rushing, rushing with no meaning. Very self-centered. Now I have a much more Dynamic Life, which I have built over the past few years to include all the things that have meaning and give me joy. It's completely different.

How was I choosing to show up? What kind of energy was I bringing into the room? We have to own that. We are responsible for it. When someone unleashes their negative energy you can feel it. So next I was to make a list of how I wanted to show up from now on. Here we go.

- Open.

- Warm.

- Friendly.

- Kind.

- Asking questions.

- Talking to everyone.

- Involved.

- Authentic.

- Engaging.

- Positive.

- Complimentary.

I try to run through a version of this list before walking into an exercise class, meeting up with friends, going to events, talking on the phone and even just going grocery shopping, anywhere I will be seeing people. Even in my own home. If I don't, it's so easy to fall into being with myself only and cutting everyone off. I can even feel when my energy is like that so I know others around me are feeling it, and that's exactly what I'm trying to avoid. Make a list of how you would like to show up in your life. Keep it somewhere you will see it until it becomes a habit to run through it mentally before engaging with others!

DAY 13 CAN YOU HEAR ME?

I used to think I was a good listener. Like a really good listener. I'm not sure why I thought this other than maybe I just seemed to be one. Deepak explains there are three levels to deep listening that allows us to be heard.

1. Listen with our ears.

2. Listen with our minds.

3. Listen with complete awareness and intimacy.

Clearly I was not doing all of that. But I notice now I find it much easier to really listen when people talk to me. I'm no longer half-listening and waiting to speak. There is a huge difference. I actually ask questions now. Before I would have just started talking when it was my turn with no recognition of what the other person just said. There is no love in that. This came naturally with the clarity that overcame me in my journey. This wasn't something that happened right when I started meditating, or stopped drinking alcohol, or when I began to feel better or any of the other things I did to better my life. It was probably a year or so into feeling good. I was driving on the highway, on my way to my yoga class, and I had a moment of pure clarity when I realized I could feel, hear and see everything differently. I felt very alive. The music I was listening to, the clouds in the sky, the sun shining, the music playing, all of it felt very different. Not only that, I was seeing life with new eyes. I was calm, happy and clear. I wondered in that moment if most people live that way on a daily basis and I was just not aware of that for a very long time. I don't know. And I don't know if it's because I'm so "clean" now—the no alcohol, no caffeine, etc.—combined with the meditation, yoga, volunteering and friendships. I'm not sure. But it was a moment of awareness I'll never forget. In my notes from this day I wrote the following:

- Pay closer attention and be present

The second part of my journaling was notes about a friend who was truly a good listener. I could learn a lot from her. She listens, asks questions and follows up with questions days later. This shows she cares. At the bottom of the page I wrote: "I want more. I have energy. I'm ready." That's powerful. Ask yourself if you are fully present when in conversation with others. What could you do to be more present for those around you?

DAY 14 I AM

STREAM OF CONSCIOUSNESS WITH THE PROMPT I AM

The goal of this exercise was to just write and let it all flow. *I am a mother, a wife, a daughter, a reader and an activist. I'm a health coach and a library aide. I'm caring. I'm a seeker. A music lover. A patron of the arts. History lover. Admirer of Gretchen Rubin, Freddie Mercury, Mick Jagger, Keith Richards, Oprah. I am an animal lover. I am pretty, strong and smart. I'm a doer. I have a lot to give and get. I feel something big, but I don't know what yet. I am a writer. I am an author of books. I am an influencer.*

It's funny what comes out when you are prompted this way. If I was to do it on my own, in my own time, the list would be much longer. I'm shocked at the number of things I left out as I am definitely more than this! But I think it's revealing that this is what came out first, on that particular day, at that particular time. It's funny to see Gretchen Rubin and Oprah lumped in with Mick, Keith and Freddie! But's just where my brain was at the moment. It's like a little poem of me. Try it!

DAYS 15-21 HANGING ON

As I finished my last 21 Day Meditation Experience I reflected on the reasons I began writing this book in the first place. On the last day Deepak said, "Letting go is a choice. If you can forgive you can trust. Clinging to the past is your separate self." And the most powerful statement to me: "Forgiveness is the natural state of a self-aware person no longer burdened by the past." Forgiveness does not come easily to me. I tend to hang on to grudges until they eat me alive. Deepak says, "When remembering the past, you relive it again. If you are present, that won't happen. Old hurts feel toxic in our expanded awareness. Forgiveness stops being a problem because there is nothing left to forgive." It took me a long time to figure out that when I stayed angry at someone for something they did, I wasn't hurting or affecting them in any way. It just made me feel angry, upset and overall just awful. I tend to be highly emotional, so everything I feel is at a very high level, the good, the bad and the ugly. I don't hide emotions well. If I'm feeling it, then pretty much everyone around me is clued in to how I feel. When I realized I could let go of those past hurts that really opened me up to how much better I could feel. And isn't that what this journey of mine is all about? Feeling the best I can and living my life? Why would I want to hang on to all that stuff? Do you ever notice how you feel when you relive a moment from your past? It's like I'm there all over again. The pain, the tears, a knot in my stomach. It's awful. There are positive outcomes to these events. I know my ability to be self-sufficient and have a strong work ethic all came out of how early I was making decisions for myself, which was when I was about eighteen years old. I didn't have many if any financial ties to my parents, so I was making all the decisions regarding college, where I lived, my health care, where I went and what I did—everything. A lot of those decisions were not good by the way! But I know my work ethic is 100 percent from how I grew up. It's not all bad! The point is not to dwell on the hurts of our past but to forgive and look for the good that may have come out of it. Do you find it difficult to forgive? Try to let go of those feelings and see how it feels.

PART 12

THE JOURNEY NEVER REALLY ENDS

I never would have guessed the road to recovery for me would end up being so much more than pain relief. I had no idea my pain was tied to anything but the injuries I was dealing with. Pain is not necessarily coming from any tissues, discs, injuries, etc. Pain comes from our brain and nervous system. Thank God I learned this or I would still be going around in circles. And that's part of the reason I wrote this book and started my blog. I am now more sure than ever that some if not most people just don't know how good they could feel. As I moved from one area of my life to another I just kept feeling better and better. Who knew life could be this good? It took working on all areas of my life: emotional, environmental, financial, intellectual, occupational, physical, social and spiritual! Everything on that wellness wheel. Every single area had lessons for me. Big lessons. I was like a little kid soaking up all the knowledge. I felt like there were all these secrets about how to live well that no one ever told me or that I ever cared to find out on my own. It took me losing just about everything to find it. I wish it hadn't taken such a horrific experience to turn myself around, but that is my story. It is clear to me I was supposed to hear this from the universe. Especially since I had to go through it twice to get my act together. I take it as a gift because if it hadn't happened I'd still be living in my old ways. I wasn't necessarily so unhappy, but I wasn't living life well and had no idea how much better it could be. My growth has been tremendous. And it doesn't end here. I'll be continuing to work on all these areas of my life to see where it all takes me. Because I've learned one thing leads to another and you never know where it will take you unless you commit to the ride.

A LITTLE AFTERWORD FUN

FAVORITE AND LIFE-CHANGING PODCASTS

Are you a podcast listener? I love podcasts. My addiction started slowly, but once I found ones I loved I became hooked. There are podcasts for any niche thing you are into. I find I would much rather spend time listening to something that really resonates with me or learning something over most (not all) of the mindless shows on television.

I have many favorites that have helped me in some way and that I've learned something from or that I just flat out find entertaining! I thought I'd share some of my favorites.

Personal Development/Health and Wellness

Happier with Gretchen Rubin/Happier in Hollywood

I'm a huge fan of her work. This show has all three of the things I was talking about. It's helped me, I've learned from it and it's entertaining. I learn little tips and tricks to use in my life and it's helped me to focus on what is important. It's where I began my second Happiness Project that set everything in motion for me and how I started my "Eighteen for 2018" lists and every year after.

Happier in Hollywood is Gretchen's sister Elizabeth's podcast that she does with her TV writing partner, Sara Fain. Its in the same vein as Happier but with the twist of life in LA as TV writers.

Balanced Bites

This one is no longer producing new episodes, but you can still access all the previous years of content. This was perfect for me when I began my paleo lifestyle. Diane Sanfilippo and Liz Wolfe are a fountain of knowledge when it comes to clean eating.

The Doctor's Farmacy with Dr. Mark Hyman

This took my knowledge of wellness and food to a whole other level. His guests are top-notch! He goes beyond just "what should we eat." He dives into climate change, farming, mindfulness, mental illness, social justice, and the list goes on. He has truly opened my eyes to the bigger picture and has inspired me to get involved with food advocacy. Future projects!

Infinite Potential with Deepak Chopra

Another teacher/mentor I have learned so much from. With all of his 21 Day Meditation Experiences I did, this was a no-brainer. Every week Deepak interviews a guest to discuss everything mind, body, spirit and beyond.

Ten Percent Happier

If you are familiar with Dan Harris from ABC News you are probably already aware of this podcast. Every week he interviews a meditation teacher or leader. I always come away inspired and motivated and I learn something new every single time.

Oprah's SuperSoul Conversations

It's Oprah! What's not to love? I'm a fan of *SuperSoul Conversations* on TV, but if I miss the episodes, I can always find them here.

The Sheri and Nancy Show

This podcast is also not producing new episodes, however if you are a woman forty or older I guarantee you will find this show not only relatable but also entertaining! Sheri spent most of her career as Oprah's producer, and now with her friend Nancy they are working on their "pillars" for all of us to hear and learn from. This show is great. It's all about the second half of life. Sheri is sixty and has no intention of slowing into retirement. What keeps you alive are all the things I talk about on my blog, and on this show they are sharing what happens as they work through them. This show gave me a total mindset shift. When I was approaching fifty, I kept thinking *I can't believe I finally figured out how to live and it's almost over.* I was sad about that for awhile, but after listening to this podcast I have a whole new attitude. When I tell people my age I also add that "I'm only halfway," and that's how I view it. I'm in the second half. After I reframed it, I now think *Wow, there's so much I want to do and I have the time to do it. Life is good.* But it doesn't magically happen on its own. If you don't work on all aspects of your life, you won't get there, or if you do you probably won't feel so great and will be forced to stop "living." Another way I've heard it described is "training for the centurion Olympics." I love that. If you want to get to 100 and feel good you absolutely must train now. Okay, that was a lot on one podcast!

Being Well with Dr. Rick Hanson

I think of Dr. Hanson as a kind of Mr. Rogers for adults. That's who he reminds me. He is so calming and extremely knowledgeable. His show focuses on mindfulness, compassion and happiness and all the science behind it. I find it fascinating.

Personal Finance

HerMoney with Jean Chatzky

You may know Jean Chatzky from the *Today Show* or *Oprah*. When I decided to get our finances in order I began listening to many personal finance podcasts. Some stuck and some didn't. This one stuck. It's informative and practical, and she always has interesting guests. I needed a lot of help in this area. I knew nothing about personal finance or money in general. I was starting at ground zero. I'm so much more literate now. This podcast was only a very small part of my learning. I went to our local library and checked out every basic personal finance book and read them all. I found a budgeting method that works for me, and now I work on our finances every single day. But the podcast keeps it in the forefront of my mind.

Music (aka podcasts that make me happy)

Disgraceland

This podcast features stories of rock stars behaving badly told by Jake Brennan. It is not for the faint of heart. Some of these stories are just outrageous. But that's what it is to be a rock star. Personally, I can't get enough.

My Favorite Album with Jeremy Dylan

This is a great concept for a music podcast. Jeremy invites musicians to discuss their favorite album song by song. It is a lot of fun to hear what these artists' favorite albums are and why.

27 Club

This is another darker podcast from Jake Brennan. This focuses an entire season on one artist who passed away at twenty-seven years old. I love a podcast that takes a deep dive and this one definitely does.

Rolling Stone Music Now

This podcast is from *Rolling Stone* magazine. It features the best interviews and music journalists in one place. I love their conversations and find myself laughing all the time.

'80s Music Exposed

This is a fun one, especially if you grew up in the '80s like me. This is a monthly podcast that discusses the albums that came out in the '80s in order by month. It's really fun to hear some of this music again and to hear the critiques. The two guys are musicians and also around my age, so I like hearing their opinions about what they liked then and now and what holds up and what doesn't.

Random

You Must Remember This

This is probably the most well done, entertaining, informative podcast I listen to. Karina Longworth hosts this podcast about old classic Hollywood. These stories are fascinating! The best part about this podcast and what makes it unique is that Karina doesn't pick random stories. She selects a subject and then goes deep. This is truly better than anything on TV. This podcast along with *Disgraceland* has won a couple of awards and you can tell why when you start listening. They are just on a different level and the work that went into them is obvious.

The Librarian Is In

The New York Public Library hosts a podcast of book recommendations and what I love about this podcast is how it is relaxed and funny, yet intelligent. I've tried other book-related podcasts and they are either stuffy or just someone reading a list of recommendations and info off the book jacket. Two employees of the library discuss one book that each of them read. The conversation always takes a turn into something else. It's just conversation. I love it. It's funny, emotional and educational. And very New York.

Clear and Vivid with Alan Alda

I've always liked Alan Alda. He is smart and funny and just seems like a great guy. I loved watching him on *MASH*. I didn't know about his interview podcast until recently. All the guests are well known, and when Alda interviews them, it's a sincere, thoughtful and intelligent conversation. It reminds me of BBC's *Desert Island Discs*.

Lost at the Smithsonian

Assif Mandvi takes listeners to the Smithsonian Museum to explain the importance of one object in the museum per episode. He interviews the staff and those who are knowledgeable about the history of the object. This one is so fun to listen to partly because Assif is so funny. One of my favorite featured objects was Henry Winkler's Fonzi jacket from *Happy Days*. Assif's interview with Henry Winkler was heartwarming. Another favorite object was Dorothy's red ruby slippers from *The Wizard of Oz*. Give it a try!

Listening to podcasts about things you are interested in or want to learn can help you achieve all your goals. By listening regularly you will keep everything that is important to you at the forefront of your mind and help you stay on track. Win-win. (As I write this I'm anxiously awaiting Brene Brown's new podcast. I can guarantee you that will be on my list!)